JOGGING
For Health and Fitness

by

Frank D. Rosato, Ed.D.
Memphis State University

Morton Publishing Company
925 W. Kenyon Ave., Unit 4
Englewood, Colorado 80110

ISBN: 0-89582-181-8

Preface

This second edition of *Jogging For Health and Fitness* has been expanded considerably. New information has replaced that which has become outdated, new trends have been identified, and the concepts presented are supported primarily by research which has occurred since the first edition was published. Every chapter in this text has been significantly affected by this revision.

The focus of this edition continues to be upon the relationship between fitness and health through the vehicle of jogging. Concomitantly, the text provides the guidelines required by a novice for starting and continuing a jogging program safely and effectively. The principles of exercise are presented, which when appropriately applied, will allow joggers to meet their fitness objectives. In addition, long-time joggers may find some of the information useful for refining their exercise program.

The author wishes to thank Lillian Fox, Beth Jensen, Piper Anderson, Betsy Spurlock, and Tom Dixon for their willingness to serve as models for the photographs. Special thanks to my daughter, Angela, for taking the photos, Lillian Fox for typing the manuscript, and Brenda Johnson for providing computer expertise.

Frank Rosato

Table of Contents

CHAPTER ONE

Introduction

AMERICA ON THE MOVE

During the past twenty years or so, we have witnessed a return to physical activity in previously sedentary America. A number of probability surveys by the Gallup and Harris organizations as well as other privately generated and government sponsored polls have indicated that the number of Americans who exercise has generally increased steadily since 1961.[1,2,3] A national survey conducted by Lieberman Research Inc. for Sports Illustrated in 1986 revealed some interesting characteristics of the present fitness movement.[4] Seven out of ten respondents reported that they participated in sports or fitness activities during the past twelve months. On the surface, this is indeed impressive but closer inspection of the data indicated that the respondents participated an average of only 53.2 times per year, or about once a week. This frequency of exercise is definitely well below the threshold required for the development of physical fitness. Only one out of ten respondents reported participating four or more times per week and twenty-seven percent of all respondents indicated that they did not participate at all in sports or physical fitness activities.

The Sports Illustrated pollsters provided a list of 34 activities ranging from very light energy expenditure to very vigorous. Table 1.1 illustrates those activities and the percentage of respondents reporting to have participated in each.

TABLE 1.1. Frequency of Participation by Activity or Sport During a 12-Month Period

Swimming	48%	Tennis	11%
Bicycling	37%	Water Skiing	10%
Fishing	35%	Snow Skiing	9%
Jogging	30%	Horseback Riding	9%
Calisthenics/Aerobics	30%	Roller Skating	9%
Using Exercise Machines	30%	Squash/Racquetball	7%
Baseball/Softball	28%	Ice Skating	5%
Bowling	23%	Sailing	5%
Hiking/Backpacking	23%	Soccer	4%
Pool/Billiards	22%	Wrestling	4%
Weight Lifting	21%	Snorkeling/Scuba Diving	3%
Boating (except sailing)	20%	Auto Racing	3%
Hunting	18%	Boxing	3%
Volleyball	16%	Track and Field Meet	2%
Basketball	15%	Ice Hockey	2%
Golf	14%	Handball	2%
Football	13%	Marathon Running	1%

Sports Illustrated. *Sports Poll '86.* Time Inc: 1986.

Plausible conclusions from all of the surveys dating back to the 1960s indicate that there has been a relative and consistent upward trend in the number of adults participating in sports and fitness activities in the last two decades. The fitness movement was spearheaded and continues to be led by persons classified as being in the middle and upper socioeconomic strata.[5] There are more men than women involved in vigorous activity and participation declines steadily with age.[4]

It is also obvious that most Americans are unaware of the proper intensity, frequency and duration of exercise needed for the development of cardiorespiratory endurance. Futhermore, many respondents participate in activities which are perceived by them as being fitness activities but which in reality, contribute either minimally or not at all to the components of fitness, such as fishing, softball, bowling, pool and billiards.[6] In fact, only ten percent of those who exercise "meet the requirements believed to prevent heart disease."[7]

The jogging/running craze has moderated to some extent in the last couple of years. Estimates of the number of active joggers vary from 30 to 35 million people.[8,9] The Brook's study[9] showed jogging to be the third most popular fitness activity following swimming and cycling. But when all activities were compared on the basis of frequency of participation, jogging ranked number one.

Race directors have indicated that participation in marathon races has declined but this has been offset by an increasing popularity of 10k (6.2 miles) races. This change has no doubt been influenced by the fact that running/jogging injuries increase in prevalence as training mileage increases.[10,11] Also contributing to the popularity of the 10k is that less time is required for training and therefore more time can be devoted to family and other interests. In addition, the training mileage required for the 10k is certainly enough to enhance cardiorespiratory health. Most adults participate in jogging for health enhancement reasons anyway — primarily to prevent heart attack or for weight loss — regardless of whether of not they compete.[5] Race competition is not a prerequisite for health enhancement or fitness, it is simply an option for those who enjoy such pursuits.

The fitness movement is evident everywhere in America. Fitness devotees are ubiquitous as people participate in jogging, swimming, cycling, aerobic dancing, roller and ice skating, skiing, racquetball, tennis and a variety of other sports and activities. In 1986, Americans spent 1.2 billion dollars for exercise equipment.[12] According to the National Sporting Goods Association, in 1986 Americans spent $424 million on stationary bikes, $217 million on rowing machines, $83 million on treadmills and $231 million on multipurpose gyms (weight training machines).[12] Accompanying the sale of exercise equipment was the purchase of athletic and sports clothing. We spent a staggering $4 billion dollars on these items. In addition, we spent another $3.2 billion on athletic footwear. Outdoor bicycles reached $1.3 billion in sales and this did not include cycling paraphernalia such as shorts, cleated shoes, gloves, helmet and shirt.

Pulse meters of different types and degrees of sophistication have been developed to monitor the intensity of exercise. Pedometers tell us how far we have travelled, and skinfold calipers tell us how much fat we have lost.

The interest in physical fitness is also reflected in the increasing amount of literature devoted to promoting health/wellness and physical fitness. Books featuring exercise of all types for fitness purposes have regularly appeared on the best-selling list. Every month popular magazines feature articles on some aspect of exercise and health. Exercise videos have become very popular regardless of the credentials and expertise of the producers of these items.

Sports drinks touted to replace the exercising body's lost nutrients are heavily advertised. It is not uncommon to see athletic teams consuming such beverages during television coverage of their games. Certain foods are hawked as energy foods and vitamin and mineral supplements are sold in large quantities also with the promise of enhancing performance.

Some advertising agencies have gone to the extreme in af- filiating with the fitness movement. Products which have nothing to do with fitness are advertised using a fitness motif. This is an eloquent commentary by those advertisers who recognize the importance of associating their products, however marginally, with the public's generally positive attitude toward fitness. The object, of course, is to transfer that positive attitude from fitness to the product which is being promoted. Whole new industries have developed around the fitness movement while others have been revitalized. Memberships in health clubs, spas, YMCA's, etc., have increased or remained steady over the last decade.

In an effort to cut escalating health care costs, many businesses and corporations have turned to fitness and wellness programs. According to the Association for Fitness in Business, American businesses paid out more than $70 billion in health care costs in 1986 and 500 million workdays were lost to illness and disability.[13] To the average person, these numbers are so large that they are incomprehensible.

To better understand the scope of these costs, we may need to look at them from the following perspective: Ten percent of a company's payroll goes to health insurance, and the health-related expenses of a typical Fortune 500 corporation are equal to twenty-four percent of its profits."[13] These are significant expenditures which are in need of reduction.

Many companies have instituted fitness and wellness programs in an effort to lower health care costs, and the early data are indeed encouraging. Containing the spiraling cost of health care seems to be worth the effort and the initial expense of developing and implementing the program.

The effects of wellness programs of which physical fitness constitutes but one component cannot be measured overnight. It takes time, effort, and an educational emphasis to change long-standing behavior patterns such as cigarette smoking, overeating, eating a high fat diet and following a sedentary lifestyle. But corporations who have implemented wellness programs have found that health care costs have been reduced, there is less worker absenteeism, there is greater productivity, less worker turnover and less on-the-job accidents.[14] Having a wellness program with fitness facilities is often used as a perk by corporations to recruit and keep key personnel.

The medical profession has become aware of the importance of regular exercise and the development and maintenance of physical fitness. A growing number of medical schools are offering courses in the physiology of exercise and a number of physicians have expressed the opinion that physicians should be able to prescribe exercise with as much skill as they prescribe medicine.

The attitude of the American public toward exercise is generally positive. Most people feel that exercise is "good for you", although many of them are not quite sure why or how it is good for you. This is probably one of the reasons why only ten to twenty percent of the exercisers are working hard enough and often enough to become physically fit. Although the exercise surveys indicate that increasing numbers of people are exercising — and this is a positive trend — a large segment of our society does not participate and a larger segment exercise at a level below that which is required to promote health and fitness. We need to continue to educate the people regarding the importance of an active lifestyle and regular exercise.

THE MECHANIZATION OF AMERICA

The fitness movement was largely a reaction to developments in science and technology and their relationship to the changing disease and death patterns in the nation. The communicable diseases (tuberculosis, pneumonia, typhoid fever, smallpox, scarlet fever, etc.) were the leading causes of death during the early years of this century. Advances in medical science have virtually eradicated these maladies and threats to life, but they have been replaced by chronic and degenerative diseases such as heart disease, stroke, cancer, diabetes, etc. This group of diseases is largely lifestyle-induced and has reached epidemic proportions.

Cardiovascular disease accounts for approximately fifty percent of all deaths in the United States. Coronary heart disease, which affects the blood vessels supplying the heart, is responsible for approximately eighty percent of heart attacks.[15] The risk factors connected with heart disease were identified by the land-mark Framingham Study which began in 1949.[16]

As the risk factors were identified there evolved the realiza-tion that heart disease was not the inevitable consequence of aging but an acquired disease that was potentially preventable. Cigarette smoking, high blood pressure, elevated levels of blood fats, diabetes, overweight, stress, lack of exercise, and a family history of heart disease were found to be highly related to heart attack and stroke. Fortunately, most of their risk factors can be modified by the way we live.

We have within our locus of control the opportunity and the right to choose what to eat and how much, whether or not to smoke cigarettes, whether or not to exercise and how we control stress. We can choose when to be screened for blood pressure and blood fats and we can choose whether or not to act upon that information. During the last two decades, millions of Americans have changed eating, smoking, and exercise habits and concomit-antly deaths from cardiovascular disease declined by approxi-mately thirty-five percent during this time. Other factors are in-volved in this favorable trend, but modifications in lifestyle have made their contribution.

Our lives today are considerably different from life in the early years of this century. Scientific and technological advances have made us functionally mechanized. Labor saving devices pro-liferate all phases of life — our occupations, home life, and leisure time pursuits — always with the promise of more and better to come. Each new invention helped foster a receptive attitude to-ward a life of ease and we have become enamoured with the easy way of doing things. The mechanized way is generally the most expedient way and in our time-oriented society, this became another stimulus for us to indulge in the sedentary life.

Today, exercise for fitness is contrived; it is programmed into our lives as an entity separate from our other functions. On the other hand, the energy expenditures of our forefathers was inte-grated and inextricably interwoven into their work, play, and home life. Physical fitness was a necessary commodity and fit people were the rule rather than the exception. Tilling the soil, digging ditches and working in factories were physically demand-ing jobs. Lumberjack contests and square dances were vigorous leisure pursuits. Being a wife and taking care of home and family required long hours at arduous tasks. In the early years of this century, one-third of the energy for operating the factories came from muscle power. By 1970, this figure dropped to less than one percent and is reflective of the declining energy demand of our jobs.

The turn of the century found seventy percent of the population working long, hard hours in the production of food. Children of this era walked several miles to school and did chores when they returned home. Today, only five percent of the population, using highly mechanized equipment, are involved in the production of food, and their children ride to school. Adults drive to the store, circle the parking lot to get as close as possible to the entrance and ride elevators and escalators while there. We mow the lawn with a riding mower, play golf in a cart, wash dishes and clothes in appropriate appliances, change television channels with a remote control, open garage doors in the same manner, and etc.

These are simply observations of life in America and are not intended to imply that the fruits of science and technology be repudiated, but rather that their results along with their impact upon us be viewed in perspective and acted upon accordingly. Mechanization has reached our leisure time and it is in this sphere that we must commit some time to vigorous activity because it has been effectively removed from other areas of life.

John Dryden recognized the seeds of change two centuries ago and wrote the following:

By chase, our long lived fathers earned their food,
Toil strung the nerves and purfied the blood.
But we, their sons, a pampered race of men,
Are dwindled down the three score years and ten,
Better to use your muscles, for health unbought,
Than fee the doctors for a nauseaous draught.
The wise, for cure, on exercise depend,
God never made his work for man to mend.

John Dryden (1631-1700)

Man has inhabited the earth for many centuries but only the last seventy-five years have generated such drastic changes in lifestyle. Our basic need for physical activity has not changed. Our bodies were constructed for, and thrive, on physical work but we find ourselves thrust into the automobile, television, and sofa age and we simply have not had enough time to adapt to this new sedentary way of living. Perhaps 100,000 years from now the sedentary life will be the healthy life. But at this stage of our development, the law of use and disuse continues to work. That which is used becomes stronger and that which is not used becomes weaker. For simple verification of this physiological principle, just witness the results of a leg in a cast for eight weeks and note the atrophy which has occurred to the limb during that time.

It is the belief of many people, this author included, that our new ways of living are precipitating or at least significantly contributing to the diseases which are affecting modern affluent man. They are unique to the highly industrialized nations. By contrast, the underdeveloped nations, with their different lifestyles, do not experience this phenomenon to the same extent.

The fitness boom had its roots in this background. The fitness movement which is occurring today started and sputtered several times during this century. World War I draft statistics indicated that many young American males were unfit for military service.[17] This prompted many states to mandate compulsory physical education, emphasizing physical development, in the public schools. When the war ended, the emphasis in these programs shifted from physical fitness to sports and games. This scenario was repeated during and after World War II.

During the mid 1950s, a fitness test which was developed for use with clinical patients, was administered to normal European and American youngsters. European youngsters scored better on the test (Kraus-Webber test) than American youngsters. This was brought to the attention of President Eisenhower who directed Vice-president Richard Nixon to investigate the problem and upgrade the fitness of American youth. Nixon's representatives contacted the American Association for Health, Physical Education, and Recreation (AAHPER) and together they established the President's Council on Youth Fitness (PCYF).

AAHPER subsequently developed the Youth Fitness Test which has been administered to American youth and national norms have been established from these data. Meanwhile, in an effort to encourage youngsters to pursue vigorous exercise, both organizations established merit awards for fitness. The AAHPER test has been revised in the last few years, and there has been one national administration of the revised test, and two of the original test. According to the results of these tests, the level of fitness of American youngsters has remained stable in the last decade and that level is considered to be sub-par. The President's

Council has changed name and focus since its inception and now encourages exercise for all Americans regardless of age.

But the greatest stimulus for an active life, particularly for adults, occurred with the publication of Kenneth Cooper's first book entitled *Aerobics*. This text literally started millions of people exercising and Cooper became — and remains — one of this country's leading spokesmen for the benefits of regular physical activity.

Although Cooper did not invent the word "aerobics," he has certainly popularized it. Aerobic exercises include walking, jogging, swimming, cycling, and rope jumping, to name but a few. These activities are performed at a comfortable pace so the participant can meet the energy demand of the exercise on a minute by minute basis for a sustained period of time. These exercises, which employ many large muscles, benefit the cardiorespiratory and muscular systems and significantly impact body composition.

FITNESS — BOOM OR BUST?

The American College of Sports Medicine (ACSM) has established criteria which should be satisfied if exercise is to meet desirable physiological and health related goals.[18] These include the following: the intensity, or vigorousness, of exercise should correspond to sixty-five to ninety percent of the maximal heart rate; this heart rate should be maintained for fifteen to sixty minutes and exercise should be pursued three to five days per week. Additionally, the ACSM suggests that beginners select from activities in which the pace can be controlled by the participant, such as walking, jogging, swimming, cycling, skating, etc. The exerciser can control the pace so as to elicit the training heart rate.

After a period of conditioning, these activities can be supplemented by games and sports for variety. Games and sports are not self-paced. Their intensity is dependent upon the skill level and motivation of the competitors.

When gauged by these criteria the results of the various surveys regarding the fitness level of the American public are far from satisfying. The fitness movement has not pervaded all segments of our society. Most of the participants in the movement are young, affluent and well educated. Secondly, the activities selected by many proclaimed exercisers, and older respondents in particular, are questionable with respect to meeting the criteria of intensity. Thirdly, the frequency of participation was well below that suggested by the ACSM. But more Americans are exercising today than at any time during the last fifty years and more are becoming aware of the importance of regular exercise. We have a long way to go, but things are looking up.

RATIONALE FOR CHOOSING JOGGING AS THE MODE OF ACTIVITY

Any activity which raises the heart rate for a sustained period of time will condition the cardiovascular system and make a positive impact upon body composition. Selection should be based upon the participant's objectives, needs, interests, and time available with some attention given to the quality of the activity. With regard to the latter, the President's Council On Physical Fitness and Sports (PCPFS) has rated jogging, cycling, and swimming as the best cardiovascular conditioners. Cross country skiing, probably the most demanding of all activities, was not evaluated in the survey.

Court games such as squash, racquetball, handball, badminton, and tennis are non-continuous activities. They consist of moderate and highly intensive bursts of energy interspersed with standing, walking and resting. The duration and intensity of these contests cannot be controlled because they are directly related to the skill and motivation of the players. Generally, the higher the level of skill, the better the workout and conversely, the poorer the skill, the poorer the workout. Optimal fitness benefits are achieved only if two highly skilled players of relatively equal ability oppose each other in singles competition. On the other hand, jogging, cycling, and swimming can be controlled with regard to pace and duration for best results. More on this in Chapter Two.

This text will concentrate upon jogging because the author, in agreement with PCPFS, considers it to be the most efficient, expedient, and inexpensive way to achieve aerobic fitness along with its attendant health benefits.

There are optimum conditions for jogging, i.e., fifty to sixty degree temperatures, humidity below twenty percent, and a resilient jogging surface. These conditions, of course, are not always available so we jog in a variety of physical and environmental conditions. But, from the standpoint of practicality, jogging can be done almost anywhere, at any time and over a variety of surfaces; this is part of its appeal for busy people.

EQUIPMENT FOR JOGGING

Shoes

The most important investment that a prospective jogger can make is the purchase of quality jogging shoes. Care should be exercised in their selection because an appropriate, well fitting pair of shoes may prevent or alleviate blisters, shin splints, ankle, knee, and hip joint injuries. See Figure 1.1.

Shoes made especially for jogging have some common characteristics. The heel should be about one-half inch higher than the sole and it should be well padded. The sole should consist of two separate layers with the outer layer made of a durable rubberized compound for traction and longevity. The inner layer should be thick and pliable and made of shock absorbing material. It is desirable for the heel and sole to flare out so the impact with the ground can be distributed over a wide area. This is critical because the jogger's foot hits the ground 600-750 times per mile with each foot strike absorbing a force equivalent to three times the body weight. It should come as no surprise that the incidence of stress injuries rises linearly with the number of miles jogged.

Flexibility, another characteristic of a good shoe, can be determined by grasping the heel in one hand and the toe in the other and bending it. If it does not bend easily, it is too stiff and inflexible for jogging.

Proper fit is another important factor. The shoes should be one-half inch longer than the longest toe and the toe box should

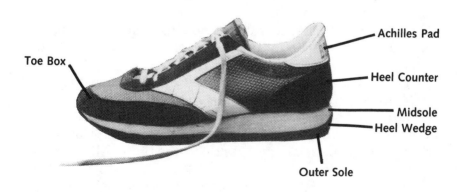

FIGURE 1.1 Typical jogging shoe.

allow enough room for the toes to spread. The toe box should be high enough not to pinch down on the toes. The heel of the foot should fit snugly in the padded heel of the shoe for maximal support and minimal friction. The shoe should have a good, firm arch support.

When purchasing a pair of shoes, one should wear the same type of sock that will be worn when jogging in order to minimize errors in sizing. Some attention should also be given to shoe maintenance. It's best to own more than one pair of shoes so they can be rotated from workout to workout. However, one pair will suffice if they are allowed to dry between workouts.

Shoes should be inspected periodically and discarded if they wear beyond the outer layer. As the shoe wears, the angle of the foot strike changes producing vectors for forces at sites in the legs and hips to which the jogger is unaccustomed. This increases the likelihood of injury and enforced idleness for a period of time.

Shoe wear can be substantially delayed. Use the shoes a few times until a pattern of wear can be observed on the heels. At this point, the jogger may apply one of many adhesive substances, which can be purchased at most sporting goods stores that carry jogging gear. These dry in twenty-four hours, can be reapplied as needed, and estimates are that they prolong the life of the shoe by 300 percent. They also insure a consistent foot plant. The vigilance and time required for repair is well worth the effort when one compares the price of the jogging shoe to the price of adhesives.

There are many excellent jogging shoes from which to select. They sell from $25 to $200 in today's market. The object is to select the best shoe for the price without going overboard, which is no easy task considering the number of makes and models available. Researchers have found that no single shoe, regardless of price, meets all criteria for orthopedic and soft tissue protection of the legs, hips and feet.

Runner's World magazine annually evaluates jogging shoes and reports the results in one of its monthly issues. This survey will acquaint you with most of the makes and models which are available and some assessment accompanies each. This survey can be a guide in helping you to select the proper shoe for your needs.

The average jogger is best served by a training shoe which weighs between ten to twelve ounces and provides maximal protection. Racing shoes weigh approximately twenty-five percent less but offer less protection. The lightest racing shoes weigh about six ounces. World class runners are willing to sacrifice protection for speed, but the jogger whose primary purpose revolves around health enhancement should select the shoe with the greatest amount of protection.

Other Gear

The selection of other gear for jogging is not as critical as that for shoes. In fact, the remainder of the outfit may be improvised and will do nicely if the clothing is loose and comfortable, does not retard the evaporation of sweat, and is appropriate for the weather. Fancy running shorts and warm-ups are unnecessary, unless one has a compulsion for fashion.

Socks, however, should be soft and absorbent and preferably made of cotton, orlon, or wool combined with nylon. You may wish to wear two pairs of socks while jogging to decrease friction and to prevent foot abrasion and blisters. In this case, one pair of socks should be a thin liner which is worn inside of a normal pair.

In warm weather, wear light colored clothing and as little as necessary within legal limits for the dissipation of heat generated by exercise. In cold weather, layers of light clothing, a hat, ear covering, gloves and possibly a ski or surgical mask will be required to protect the jogger.

SUMMARY

Advances in science, technology, and nutrition have helped to produce an overweight and underexercised population. While wholesale changes were occurring in lifestyle during this century concomitant changes were also being observed in disease patterns and causes of death with the chronic diseases supplanting the communicable diseases as the leading killers of Americans.

Jogging is an exceptionally good activity for the development of cardiovascular endurance and an important catalyst for producing favorable body composition changes. Jogging is a versatile activity which can be done alone, with a partner or group, is relatively inexpensive, can take place almost anywhere at any time, can be competitive or enjoyed for fun, and requires a minimum amount of equipment.

REFERENCES

1. Perrier Great Water of France, Inc. "Perrier Study: Fitness In America." New York: Perrier, 1979
2. Haskell, W. L., Montoye, H. J., and Orenstein, D. "Physical Activity and Exercise to Achieve Health-Related Physical Fitness Benefits," *Public Health Reports,* 100:202, 1985.
3. Schoenborn, C. A. "Health Habits of U. S. Adults 1985: The "Alameda 7" Revisited," *Public Health Reports,* 101:571, 1986
4. Sports Illustrated. *Sports Poll '86,* Time Inc: 1986.
5. Blair, S. N., Mulder, R. T. and Kohl, H. W. "Reaction to 'Secular Trends In Adult Physical Activity: Exercise Boom or Bust'?", *Research Quarterly For Exercise and Sport,* 58:No. 2, 106, 1987.
6. Simmons, K. "The Federal Government: Keeping Tabs on the Nation's Fitness", *The Physician and Sportsmedicine,* 15:No. 1, 190, January, 1987.
7. Cinque, C. "Are Americans Fit? Survey Data Conflict", *The Physician and Sportsmedicine,* 14:No. 11, 24, November, 1986
8. McBryde, A. M. and others. "Injuries In Runners and Joggers", in Schneider, R. C. and others (eds.): *Sports Injuries: Mechanisms, Prevention and Treatment,* Baltimore: Williams and Williams, 1985.
9. Brooks, C. M. "Adult Participation In Physical Activities Requiring Moderate to High Levels of Energy Expenditure", *The Physician and Sportsmedicine,* 15:No. 9, 118, April, 1987

10. Koplan, J. P. and others. "An Epidemiological Study of the Benefits and Risks of Running", *Journal of the American Medical Association,* 248:3118, December 17, 1982.
11. Blair, S. N. "Risk Factors and Running Injuries", *Medicine and Science in Sports and Exercise,* 17(2):XII, 1985.
12. Schaefer, C. "The Price You'll Pay to Sweat", *Changing Times,* 41:No. 8, 38, August, 1987.
13. Gambaccini, P. "The Bottom Line On Fitness", *Runner's World,* 66, July, 1987.
14. AFB. "American Business Gets Fit", *Business Week,* 1, October 7, 1985.
15. *Reduce Your Risk of Heart Attack,* American Heart Association, 1981.
16. Kannell, W. B. and others. "Epidemiology of Acute Myocardial Infarction: The Framingham Study", *Medicine Today,* 2:50, 1968.
17. Anderson, G. F. "A Period of Projects 1955-1980", *Journal of Physical Education, Recreation and Dance,* 56:No. 4, 72, April, 1985.
18. American College of Sports Medicine. *Guidelines For Exercise Testing and Prescription (3rd Edition),* Philadelphia: Lea and Fabiger, 1986.

CHAPTER TWO

Guidelines
For Jogging

Jogging should become a lifelong activity if it is to make a significant and lasting impact upon our state of health. A sound program based upon the guidelines and suggestions presented in this chapter has the capacity to improve the quality of one's life. The benefits associated with consistent participation will be discussed in a later chapter. For now, concentrate on starting your program correctly.

STARTING OUT RIGHT

To be effective, jogging or any other exercise must be pursued on a regular basis. Regular participation for two or three months will yield a variety of physiological, psychological and health benefits which may ultimately provide the motivation for continuation. The problem for the beginning jogger is to sustain the program during the early weeks without becoming bored or incurring an injury. Enthusiastic beginners, anxious to achieve their goals rapidly, tend to overdo in the early days of the fitness program. Beginning joggers are faced with a "catch 22" situation: they need enthusiasm to start the program but too much enthusiasm may stimulate them to exercise beyond their capability thus increasing the likelihood of injury. Jogging at a level beyond one's capability is extremely uncomfortable. Heart rate will be elevated above the recommended level, breathing becomes labored, muscles will ache and there will be no enjoyment of the activity. Stiffness and soreness the day after will add to the discomfort. If the jogger continues in this manner, a negative attitude toward jogging will quickly develop and soon the program, along with all of its good intentions, will be discarded. After all, how many of us are masochistic enough to endure the pain until we become fit enough to overcome it? Probably not many. There must be some enjoyment of the activity in order for it to be sustained for a lifetime. For normal people, pain and enjoyment are contradictory feelings — they don't fit together. So, it is important to understand and follow the principles that are discussed in this chapter. If you adhere to these principles, you will probably learn to enjoy jogging, you will receive many benefits, and you will significantly decrease the probability of incurring an injury.

MEDICAL EXAM

The American College of Sports Medicine (ACSM) has established exercise guidelines for apparently healthy individuals, individuals at higher risk, and patients with disease.[1] Apparently healthy people under the age of 45 can engage in regular exercise without an exercise tolerance test. However, they should begin and proceed gradually and they should be able to recognize unusual signs or symptoms which appear to be exercise induced. Those who are 45 or older are advised to take a physician monitored maximal exercise test prior to starting an exercise program.

"Individuals at higher risk are those with at least one major coronary risk factor and/or symptoms suggestive of cardiopulmonary or metabolic disease."[1] The major risk factors include high blood pressure, cigarette smoking, elevated cholesterol, abnormal electrocardiogram, family history of heart disease and diabetes. Metabolic diseases include diabetes, liver or kidney disease and thyroid disorders. People who exhibit one or more of these should have an exercise test regardless of age.

"Individuals at any age with known cardiovascular, pulmonary, or metabolic disease should have an exercise test prior to beginning vigorous exercise."[1] For these people, an exercise test is necessary to determine whether the benefits of exercise outweigh the risk. Secondly, it is important to measure functional capacity for later comparison.

THE JOGGER'S AIMS AND OBJECTIVES

The jogger's aims and objectives should dictate the direction and type of program to be pursued. Programs designed for individuals who desire to lose weight would be significantly different than those which may be developed for road race competition. If such programs are properly conceived, the objectives would be reflected by the manner that the principles of intensity, frequency and duration are manipulated by the participant. The degree to which each of these factors is emphasized or deemphasized is the key to accomplishing specific objectives.

TRAINING PRINCIPLES

Intensity

Intensity refers to the degree of vigor associated with each bout of exercise — in this case, jogging. Research data support the notion that an intensity level equivalent to 60 percent of the aerobic capacity is the threshold above which a cardiovascular training effect occurs. By the same token, 80 percent of the aerobic capacity is recognized as the upper limit of exercise. Therefore, it follows that the intensity of jogging need not be maximal for a training effect to occur. This rather nicely dispels the cherished myth that jogging must be painful to be beneficial. Individuals who cannot carry on a conversation without gasping for breath between each word are performing at a pace which is too vigorous for their fitness level. This is a good subjective test which lessens the probability of overexertion; however, it doesn't indicate whether the jogger is exercising at the level needed for the achievement of optimal results. A more precise method utilizes the heart rate for calculating the upper and lower limits for jogging. Seventy percent of maximal heart rate is roughly equivalent to 60 percent of the aerobic capacity and 85 percent of maximal heart rate is about equal to 80 percent of the aerobic capacity. These are well within ACSM guidelines and quite appropriate for young, healthy, but untrained adults.

Maximal heart rate is accurately determined by an all-out treadmill or bicycle ergometer test. Formulas based on thousands of these work capacity tests have been developed to estimate maximal heart rate for the average person who does not have access to these sophisticated procedures. The formulas predict rather than assess so there is some measurement error associated with their use. The error factor must be considered when developing the exercise prescription.

The error of measurement for maximal heart rate has been estimated to be a minimum of ten beats per minute. Therefore, five percent of any given age group could be as much as 20 beats over or under the predicted max and another 27 percent would be expected to vary from 11 to 19 beats in either direction. These are conservative estimates. See Figure 2.1.

FIGURE 2.1 Possible error associated with predicting max, H.R.

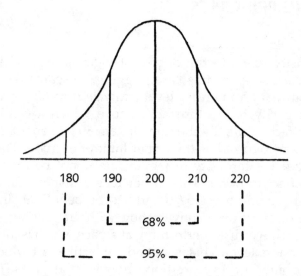

This figure indicates that 68 percent of the 20 year olds will have a max. H.R. between 190-210, 95 percent will be between 180 and 220 and the other 5 percent will be above or below these heart rate values.

The safety implications for prescribing exercise based on target heart rate are substantial. A significant deviation from average would result in misjudgment of the individual's tolerance for exercise. The greater risk of the two is associated with overestimating the prospective jogger's limits resulting in a pace which is initially too strenuous.

The calculations involved in determining maximal heart rate and exercise target heart rates for a 20 year old are as follows:

$$\begin{array}{l} 220 \ (\text{a constant}) \\ \underline{-20 \ (\text{age})} \\ 200 \ (\text{Max. H.R. beats/min}) \end{array}$$

$$\begin{array}{cc} 200 \ (\text{Max. H.R.}) & 200 \ (\text{Max. H.R.}) \\ \underline{\times .70 \ (\% \ \text{Max. H.R.})} & \underline{\times .85 \ (\% \ \text{Max. H.R.})} \\ 140 \ (\text{beats/min}) & 170 \ (\text{beats/min}) \end{array}$$

A heart rate of 140 beats per minute represents 60 percent of the aerobic capacity or the lower limit of the exercise training zone: a heart rate of 170 beats per minute represents 80 percent of the aerobic capacity or the upper limit of the training zone. It is desirable to select a ten beat range within this continuum as the target zone for jogging. A sedentary 20 year old would select the lower end of the continuum (140-150 beats/min) as the target zone while a better conditioned individual (same age) would choose a value closer to the upper end. The sedentary person would move the target zone in the direction of the upper portion of the continuum as fitness improved and his/her needs dictated.

The beauty of this system is that the level of fitness can improve even when the target zone remains static. That is, the heart rate for a given work load declines as fitness improves so a lesser percentage of the aerobic capacity is required to do the same amount of work. For instance, jogging at a ten-minute-mile pace may elicit the target zone heart rate in the early days of the program. But, as fitness improves the pace will need to be quickened to reach the target heart rate. Improvements will continue as the participant jogs faster and longer all within the same target zone. Of course, remaining at the lower end of the continuum will limit the potential for cardiorespiratory improvement but the jogger's objectives may not require maximal aerobic status. In this case, it is not necessary to move the target zone upward.

The formula for calculating the target zone for exercise applies reasonably well up to age 65 or 70. Simply follow the steps in the previous example or refer to Figure 2.2 which provides by inspection the max heart rate and the training heart rates for various ages. Maximal heart rate declines with age and so

FIGURE 2.2   Maximal and target zone heart rates.

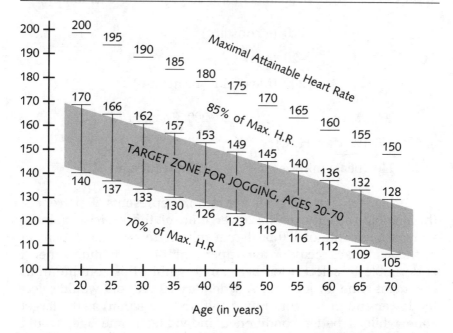

Age (in years)

This figure expresses average values by age for maximal attainable heart rate during an all-out effort. This value decreases approximately one beat/minute per year after age 20. Target zone heart rates decline correspondingly.

does the target zone for exercise. Maximal heart rate declines about one beat per year after age 20 and up to 65 or 70. After 70, it declines less than one beat per year. Cooper suggests that active older people should use 205 minus one-half their age to determine the maximal heart rate and then multiply that value by 60-70 percent to find a reasonable training zone.[2]

Learning to take pulse rate is a skill that one must develop in order to determine if the heart rate is within the prescribed zone. There are several sites in the body where the pulse can be felt, but the most practical for the jogger is the radial pulse located in the wrist at the base of the thumb while the hand is held palm up. The carotid pulse can be felt in the large arteries at either side of the neck. This may not be an appropriate site for estimating exercise heart rate because excessive pressure on these arteries stimulates a circulatory reflex which slows the heart thus underestimating exercise intensity.

The pulse should be palpated with the first three fingers, not the thumb. To figure exercise heart rate, the jogger should periodically stop jogging, immediately count the pulse rate for ten seconds, multiply this figure by six to obtain heart rate per minute. The first pulse sound should be counted as "zero." It is imperative that the count be started immediately upon cessation of jogging to get an accurate indication of exercise heart rate due to its rapid decline when activity ceases. See Figure 2.3.

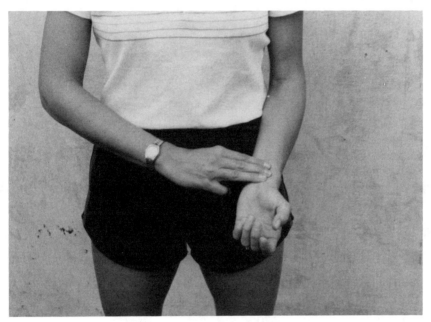

FIGURE 2.3   Taking pulse rate at the wrist.

Monitoring exercise by heart rate is generally an effective method but it is not without flaws. First, stopping to take pulse rates becomes tedious and tends to interrupt the workout. Second, unless the maximum heart rate is assessed by an exercise tolerance test there is the possibility of substantial error. Third, it might encourage slavish dependence upon heart rate to the exclusion of perceived exertion or one's subjective impression regarding how difficult the workout feels. It is important that you tune into your body and that you learn to recognize and pay attention to the signals it gives. Some of the notable signals that form our perception of exertion during exercise include rate and depth of breathing, heart rate, body temperature, musculoskeletal stress and pain, and overall discomfort. Gunnar Borg has developed a rating scale that predicts actual exercise heart rate quite accurately.[3] This scale is presented in Figure 2.4.

FIGURE 2.4   The Perceived Exertion Scale.

This scale and the target heart rate during exercise are excellent ways to monitor physical activity.

6	
7	Very, Very Light
8	
9	Very Light
10	
11	Fairly Light
12	
13	Somewhat Hard
14	
15	Hard
16	
17	Very Hard
18	
19	Very, Very Hard
20	

You will note that the scale ranges from 6 to 20, with 6 being very, very light and 20 corresponding to very, very hard. When multiplied by a factor of 10, the numbers on the scale represent heart rates. A rating of 6 is translated as a heart rate of 60 and a rating of 20 is translated as a heart rate of 200. Published data indicate that the rating of perceived exertion not only correlates quite well with actual exertion as exhibited by exercise heart rate, but is oftentimes a better criterion measure since it considers more than just the exercise heart rate.[4] It encompasses sensory input from all of the systems associated with the generation of energy for movement.

Perceived exertion is an excellent technique for monitoring exercise, particularly when maximal heart rate is estimated. If the heart rate maximum is overestimated, so too will the exercise target rate. Perceived exertion may be used to compensate for the error, thus averting overwork and its consequences. Also, we all experience days when exercise is more difficult. As Dishman stated, ". . . there are days when the track just seems longer, and the hills are definitely steeper."[5] Much like a sputtering auto engine, our body is trying to tell us something. When we experience such feelings we should adjust the intensity downward and shorten the duration of the workout instead of pressing on as usual. Tomorrow will probably be a better day. The point is that we should not neglect what our body is attempting to communicate and we should capitalize upon this source of feedback to make adjustments when needed.

Duration

Duration and intensity are inversely related; the more intense the exercise the shorter its duration and vice versa. For novices and health runners, it is best to sacrifice some degree of intensity for duration. The caloric difference between jogging a mile in seven minutes or nine minutes is insignificant, so jogging a little extra time or distance at a slower pace is more comfortably tolerated. In essence, the total amount of work done as measured by calories expended appears to be the salient factor in achieving the health benefits of exercise. Three hundred calories per session seem to be the lower limit for their attainment. This translates roughly into three miles of jogging. For a more accurate estimate, see Appendix A.

Each workout should last from 15 to 60 minutes exclusive of warm-up and cool-down. Jogging, which is prolonged beyond 60 minutes, produces diminishing returns for the extra time invested and increases the chances of injury. Programs lasting longer than 60 minutes may be necessary for competitors, but not health runners.

Workouts of short duration (15-20 minutes) should feature higher intensities than workouts of longer duration (40-60 minutes) in order to achieve similar fitness effects. The type of workout, high intensity or long duration, is generally selected by such factors as the fitness objectives to be met, the amount of time available for exercise, and the training preference of the exerciser.

Frequency

The ACSM indicates that three to five days of exercise per week is sufficient for producing a training effect. As with other principles of exercise, the frequency of jogging will vary with the jogger's objectives. Those interested in weight loss and altering body composition as well as those who are primarily interested in stress reduction would do well to jog five or possibly six days per week, whereas three to four days per week would suffice for a lean individual who is concerned with the development of more energy and endurance.

Low intensity exercise of moderate duration (20-40 minutes), such as walking, could be pursued every day without producing physiological or orthopedic problems, but high-intensity, longer-duration exercises such as jogging, biking, aerobic dancing, and the like need to be performed only three to five days per week. Days of rest are an important part of the training programs of people who exercise for health-related reasons — even world class competitive athletes need to take an occasional day off to recharge the physiological and psychological batteries. Rest days should be spaced rather than taken consecutively. However, the results of one study indicated that three consecutive days of exercise followed by four days of rest produced a training effect that was similar to a program featuring alternate days of work and rest.[6] A regimen such as this is not preferred because the cardiovascular and fitness benefits of exercise begin to regress 48 to 72 hours after the last bout. Two weeks of inactivity produce a significant reduction in exercise capacity and ten weeks to eight months without exercise will return the individual to pretraining levels.[7]

Exercise should be performed at least every other day to maintain fitness. Also, data indicate that triglyceride levels in the blood are reduced for 48 to 72 hours subsequent to the last bout of aerobic exercise. Keeping this risk factor for heart disease continuously suppressed requires that the next exercise session occur prior to the elapse of that time. Periodic rest days also make sense in regard to lowering the likelihood of incurring an injury and combating the possibility of becoming "stale." There is a fine line between the amount of exercise that produces maximum gains and the amount that results in the negative effects (staleness) associated with overtraining. Overtraining occurs when exercisers do too much too often. The signs of this phenomenon are:

1. A feeling of chronic fatigue and listlessness.
2. Inability to make further fitness gains (or there may be a loss of fitness).
3. A sudden loss of weight.
4. An increase of five beats or more in the resting heart rate, taken in the morning prior to getting out of bed.
5. Loss of enthusiasm for working out (the exerciser no longer looks forward to the workout).

Staleness may be both psychological (lack of variety in the program or boredom after years of training) and physiological. It is probably a combination of both, but the treatment is the same: either stop training for a few days to a few weeks (depends upon the severity of staleness) or cut back substantially. In either case, rebuild and regain fitness gradually. Prevention is the best treatment. Recognize the signs and adjust accordingly before staleness becomes a problem.

The relationship among intensity, duration and frequency has been studied extensively. After reviewing the literature, this author recommends that the intensity of jogging be approximately 75 to 80 percent of the maximal heart rate, last for 30 to 60 minutes, and take place four to five times per week. This schedule insures that a training effect will occur in relative comfort, and maximum safety, while meeting the objectives of most health runners.

Progression and Overload

When people attain a level of fitness which meets their needs and satisfies their objectives and further improvement is no longer desired, the program switches from the development of fitness to the maintenance of fitness. The principles of progression and overload are no longer needed at this point, but both are extremely important during the development or improvement phase of the program. Overload involves subjecting the various systems of the body to gradual and unaccustomed stresses. It is only through overload that the body adapts and improvement occurs; without it, no adaptation or improvement takes place.

The principle of progression actually functions as the schedule for the application of overload. The key to overloading the body is to apply stress slowly and progressively but only when it is warranted and not before. Overloading too soon will probably culminate in injury to both body and ego. Be realistic — exercise is a lifetime endeavor; there's plenty of time for improvement. Slow down, enjoy it, and do not tear grimly and hastily through the exercise session. From a health standpoint, exercise is as important as anything you will do during the day, so give it the attention that any important and necessary activity deserves.

In jogging, overload is applied by increasing the distance or decreasing the time required to cover the distance. Target heart rate and perceived exertion can be used to indicate the appropriate time to apply overload. For example, if a jogger is capable of covering five miles in fifty minutes but aspires to cover that distance in 35 minutes, he/she must apply a systematic progression of overload. Further, this individual is currently able to jog five miles with a heart rate ranging from 150 to 160 beats per minute. Adaptations resulting from training will, over a short period of time, reduce the heart rate below 150 beats per minute. It is at this time that the speed should be increased to force the heart rate back into the target zone. Further adaptations will reduce the heart rate and necessitate greater running speed. This process will continue in an alternating manner until the jogger reaches the objective. However, the greatest adaptations or improvements (training effect) occur in the early weeks and months of training and slow down as training continues. As one reaches his/her maximal potential, improvements occur by small increments but continue to do so for many years.

Three observations might be noted regarding the application of overload and progression: patience is required, improvement occurs in small increments, and most importantly, improvements should occur only when certain criteria are met indicating that the individual is ready to attempt a newer challenge.

There is ample evidence to support the contention that the body adapts according to the specific type of stress placed upon it. The muscles used in any given activity are the ones that adapt and they do so in the specific way in which they are used. Jogging does not prepare one for swimming and swimming does not prepare one for cycling. The legs are stressed in jogging in a manner indigenous to that activity. Those adaptations which occur from jogging provide very little carry-over to the leg kick for swimming.

Warming Up

Warming up, or getting the body ready for exercise, is one of the often slighted and sometimes neglected phases of a workout. The muscles of the legs, buttocks, and lower back are strengthened and shortened through jogging. This can have a profound negative effect upon posture, and the imbalances produced between the muscles in these areas (agonists) and their antagonists (muscles which must relax while agonists contract) create a greater susceptibility to injury. Stretching exercises are employed to counteract this phenomenon. Warm-up may be passive, active or a combination of the two. Passive activities include massage, steam or sauna, hot towels, and whirlpool baths. These might alleviate the stiffness and soreness that may carry over from the previous workout. A passive warm-up might be an adjunct to, but not a replacement for, an active warm-up prior to exercise.

An active warm-up usually includes a general and a specific component. The general component consists of stretching and large muscle activities designed to slowly raise the heart rate while increasing muscle temperature.

Static stretching is the preferred method for enhancing and maintaining flexibility and suppleness. This involves slow stretching, holding terminal positions for 15 to 30 seconds, and then repeating the movement at least one more time. Muscles should be stretched slowly and progressively to the point of discomfort, not pain. This method does not stretch the tissues beyond their limits, is economical in terms of energy expenditure, helps prevent muscle soreness, and alleviates soreness should it already exist.

Static stretching should be preceded by large muscle activities such as rhythmic calisthenics, running in place and slow jogging. These activities raise muscle temperature and gently raise the heart rate toward that expected during the exercise session. An increase in muscle temperature facilitates muscular stretch, effecting an increase in flexibility in the long term and is less likely to result in injury. See Figures 2.5 through 2.10 for some typical stretching exercises suggested for joggers.

Dynamic stretching, consisting of bouncing movements, has been largely discarded because it invokes specialized receptors located in the muscles which respond to fast bouncing movements. When these receptors are stimulated, the muscles being

FIGURE 2.5 Modified Hurdler's Stretch. Sit on the floor and fully extend the left leg. Bend the right knee and place the sole of the right foot against the left thigh. Lean forward, keep the left leg straight and attempt to reach the toes with extended left hand. Hold 15 to 30 seconds and switch legs. Stretches the hamstring group.

FIGURE 2.6 Modified Hurdler's Stretch. Similar to Figure 2.5 except that you reach forward with the opposite hand. This will place some stretch upon the low back as well as the hamstrings. Hold 15 to 30 seconds and switch legs.

FIGURE 2.7 Back Stretcher. Lie on your back and pull both knees into the chest. Stretches lower back. Hold 15-30 seconds.

FIGURE 2.8 Thigh Stretcher. Place left hand against a wall for support and grasp the toes of the right foot and pull that foot toward the buttocks. Do not lean forward. Stretches the front of the thigh. Hold 15 to 30 seconds and switch legs.

FIGURE 2.9 Achilles Tendon Stretch. Support your weight by leaning against a wall. Bend your knees, keep your feet flat on the floor and lean forward until a stretch is felt in the achilles tendons and calves. Hold 15 to 30 seconds.

FIGURE 2.10 Achilles Tendon Stretcher. Assume a stride position with the forward leg bent at the knee and the rear leg straight with heel planted down firmly. Lean forward until discomfort is felt in the achilles tendon and calf muscle. Hold 15-30 seconds.

stretched actually contract, counteracting the effect of the stretching routine. The simultaneous action of stretching and contraction
in the same muscles produces soreness and possible injury to
muscle tissue. These receptors are not stimulated by slow static
stretching.

A second aspect of a general warm-up includes such activities
as rhythmic calisthenics and running in place or slow jogging.
These are designed to raise the heart rate gently toward that expected during the workout. In the absence of warming up, the
heart rate would escalate rapidly from the resting to the performing state. But circulation would lag behind, resulting in a brief
interval when the heart could not be supplied with its increased
demand for oxygen and nutrients. During this period, the heart
muscle is laboring without an adequate supply of fuel. The
healthy, well-conditioned heart can endure such treatment, but
nevertheless there is an element of risk. One study indicated that
44 healthy male subjects, ages 21-52, had normal electrocardio-
graphic (ECG) responses to exercise which followed a warm-up
consisting of two minutes of easy jogging, but 31 of them (70
percent) developed abnormal ECG responses to the same exercise
when it was not preceded by warming up.[8] Another reason usually given to justify warming up properly is that muscles contract
faster when heated which may improve performance and prevent
injury.

The specific component of warming up involves participation
in the activity to be performed or a related activity. For example,
subsequent to the completion of the general phase of warm up,
joggers might run in place or jog the first half mile of the workout
at a leisurely pace slowly increasing to the desired speed. In this
way, the body is allowed to selectively and gradually adapt to the
specific stress to be imposed upon it. The concepts of general and
specific warm up apply to most activities — swimming, biking,
rope jumping, racquetball, tennis, and many others.

Cool Down

Cooling down from exercise is as important as warming up.
Just as the body was allowed to speed up gradually, it must also
be allowed to slow down gradually. The body is not analogous to
an auto engine that can be turned on and off with the twist of a
key. Cool-down should last about 8 to 10 minutes. The first phase
of cooling down should consist of walking or some other light

activity to prevent blood from pooling in the active muscles. Five minutes of continuous light activity causes rhythmical muscle contractions that prevent the pooling of blood and helps to move blood back to the heart for redistribution to the vital organs. This boost to circulation after exercise is an essential component of the cool-down period. Inactivity during this time forces the heart to compensate for the reduced volume of blood returning to it by maintaining a high pumping rate. The exerciser runs the risk of dizziness, fainting, and perhaps more serious consequences associated with diminished blood flow. Light activity also speeds up the removal of lactic acid which has accumulated in the muscles.

The second phase of cool-down should focus upon the same stretching exercises that were used during the warm-up period. You will probably note that stretching is tolerated more comfortably after exercise due to the increase in muscle temperature. Stretching at this time helps prevent muscle soreness. Bent leg sit-ups should be added to the routine. Strong abdominal muscles are a postural aid because they provide support for the upper torso. Modified sit-ups should be done by those who cannot do sit-ups correctly due to unused and weak abdominals. Correct performance requires that the back be rounded as the participant sits up. See Figures 2.11 through 2.14.

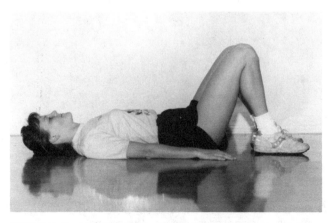

FIGURE 2.11 Modified Sit-Up, Part 1. Lie on your back with knees bent and heels close to the buttocks. This is the starting position.

FIGURE 2.12 Modified Sit-Up, Part 2. Curl up until your fingertips contact your knees and return to the starting position. This is a good lead-up to sit-ups. Start with 10 repetitions and progress from there.

FIGURE 2.13 Sit-Up, Part 1. Lie on your back, knees bent, feet close to buttocks, arms folded across chest. This is the starting position.

FIGURE 2.14 Sit-Up, Part 2. Curl up until your elbows touch your knees and return to the starting position. Start with 10 repetitions and progress from there. This is more difficult than the modified sit-up.

Many people who exercise in health clubs finish off a workout by taking a steam or sauna bath. This is potentially hazardous because the body heat generated during the workout cannot be removed. In fact, the temperature in the steam or sauna room is substantially higher than human body temperature so the exerciser will absorb heat from the environment and this will be added to the heat which has accumulated during exercise. Secondly, the exerciser has lost body fluid during exercise and will continue to do so in a steam or sauna. There is not much advantage to taking a steam or sauna bath, but if one must, then he or she should cool down sufficiently after exercise and replace the fluid which was lost during the workout prior to a steam or sauna bath.

Jogging Form

A comfortably erect posture with head up and eyes level encourages correct body alignment for jogging. See Figures 2.15 and 2.16. The eyes should be focused twenty to twenty-five feet down

FIGURE 2.15 Correct jogging form.

FIGURE 2.16 Correct jogging form.

the road rather than in front of the feet. The hands, which are loosely closed, should be carried lower than the elbows for energy conservation and comfort. This posture tends to relax the neck and shoulders. The low hand position mitigates against the generation of powerful pumping action from the arms, but this is not necessary for jogging. Sprinters require power from the arm swing; joggers swing the arms for rhythm and balance. The arms should be swung backward and forward but should not cross in front of the body.

The jogging stride should be short and compact with the foot landing beneath the knee. This is an aid to keeping the body erect and prevents overstriding. The jogger should land softly on the heel and rock up through the ball of the foot to the toes for the push-off. The body weight transfers from the heel, along the outside edge of the foot to the toes. This distributes the impact over a greater surface area and for a longer period of time and results in smooth energy-efficient locomotion. The landing should be essentially noiseless. See Figure 2.17. Many beginners, particularly

FIGURE 2.17   Correct footstrike.

those who have played competitive baseball, basketball, and football, tend to land first on the ball of the foot. This footstrike is inappropriate for distance running because the relatively small muscles of the lower leg absorb the majority of the force, whereas the heel landing stresses the larger muscles of the upper leg. Flatfooted landing represents a compromise between the two. It is better than landing on the ball of the foot but not as good as landing on the heel.

Up and down and side to side movements while jogging should be avoided because they result in inefficient technique which wastes energy. For best results, all of the energy generated should be directed toward smooth horizontal motion.

JOGGING IN HOT AND COLD WEATHER

Human beings are compelled to function in a variety of environmental conditions. People live and work in frigid, temperate, and tropical zones, at sea level and at high altitudes and have adapted and learned to tolerate extremes in temperature. In cold weather, body temperature may be maintained by putting on more clothes or by increasing the body's production of heat through physical movement or shivering. In hot environments heat may be lost through sweating, increasing blood flow to the skin, and by wearing as little clothing as the law and culture will allow.

Humans are homeotherms (meaning "same heat") who are capable of maintaining the constant internal temperature necessary for the support of such life-sustaining processes as cellular metabolism, oxygen transport, muscular contraction, etc. We exist within a relatively narrow band of internal temperature, ranging from 97 to 99 degrees, but our temperature may (and often does) rise to 104 degrees during exercise. Temperatures that rise above 106 degrees, if not rapidly reduced, often result in cellular deterioration, permanent brain damage, and death; while temperatures below 93 degrees slow metabolism to the extent that unconsciousness and cardiac arrhythmias (disturbances of normal heart rhythm that can be fatal) are likely.

Mechanisms of Heat Loss

Heat is generated in the body at rest and during exercise, as a by-product of all of its biochemical reactions. Metabolism is the collective sum of these reactions. Exercise stimulates metabolism and increases the amount of heat produced. Heat developed during exercise is positively related to its intensity and duration.

The efficiency of the body's machinery in the production of energy is considerably less than 100 percent; in fact, it varies from ten to thirty percent depending upon the type of activity being performed. The majority of the energy produced to support physical activity is lost in the form of heat. This creates a substantial heat load in the body that must be dissipated for the safety of the participant. During exercise, the body's adaptive mechanisms, which are centered upon shunting blood to the skin, are mobilized for this purpose. The processes of heat removal involve conduction, radiation, convection, and the evaporation of sweat.

Conduction is the transfer of heat from the body to an object by means of physical contact between the two. Sitting in a chair or pressing one's back against a wall will transfer heat from the body to either object. Conduction contributes little to heat loss during most types of physical activity, but swimming is a notable exception.

Radiation involves the transference of heat from the body to the atmosphere by electromagnetic waves, provided the environmental temperature is below a skin temperature of 92 to 93 degrees. Heat travels on a temperature gradient from a warmer to a cooler object so the greater the difference between skin and environmental temperatures the greater the heat loss through radiation. Radiation occurs in the reverse direction when the environmental temperature is above skin temperature and the participant absorbs heat from the environment.

Convection involves the transference of heat from the body to a moving gas or liquid. Heat loss through convection occurs more rapidly and efficiently when the wind is blowing. Heat that is transmitted to the surrounding air is blown away, allowing for the additional transfer of heat to the newer surrounding air. Heat loss by convective processes occurs even more rapidly in the water.

The major means of ridding the body of the heat generated by exercise is through the evaporation of sweat. This mechanism is effective even in high temperatures provided the relative humidity is low. If both the temperature and humidity are high it is difficult to lose heat by any of these processes. Under these circumstances it is best to adjust the intensity and duration of exercise or to move the program indoors where the temperature and humidity can be controlled.

Jogging in Hot Weather

Hot, humid days present by far the greatest climatic challenge to the enthusiast who exercises outdoors. Humid air is very saturated with moisture, and cannot absorb much more, so sweat produced during exercise beads up and rolls off the body, providing very little cooling effect. More blood than usual is diverted from the muscles to the skin in an effort to carry the heat accumulating in the deeper recesses of the body to its outer surface. The net result is that the exercising muscles are deprived of a full complement of blood and cannot work as long or as hard at a given task.

The high sweat rates which accompany vigorous exercise during hot and humid conditions promote the loss of a sizeable quantity of the body's fluid, some of which comes from the bloodstream. The blood becomes more viscous (sticky), lessening its ability to deliver oxygen to the active muscles. Fluid lost from the body is accompanied by the loss of the electrolytes sodium and potassium. If the participant continues to exercise strenuously, body temperature will rise and may exceed the capacity of the temperature-regulating mechanisms to remove heat. Heat exhaustion or heat stroke occurs with the breakdown of the body's temperature-regulating mechanisms. Both conditions require immediate first aid, but heat stroke is a medical emergency that poses an imminent threat to life. It is the most severe of the heat-induced illnesses. The symptoms include a high temperature (106 degrees F or higher), generally the absence of sweating, and dry skin. Delirium, convulsions, and loss of consciousness often occur. The early warning signs include chills, nausea, headache, general weakness, and dry skin. The victim should be rushed to the nearest hospital immediately because death will probably occur without appropriate early treatment. Heat exhaustion, a serious condition but not an imminent threat to life, is characterized by dizziness, fainting, rapid pulse, and cool skin. The victim should be moved to a shady area or indoors, placed in a reclining position, and given cool fluids to drink.

Successful performance in a hot environment is dependent upon the temperature, humidity, air movement, the intensity and duration of exercise, the individual's level of fitness, previous exposure to heat (acclimatization) and whether the workout occurs in direct sunlight. Caution should be exercised when the temperature exceeds 83 degrees F and the humidity rises above sixty percent. Sharkey has developed the following standards for work or exercise in hot weather:

1. Use discretion when the temperature is above 80 degrees F
2. Avoid strenuous activity when the temperature is above 85 degrees F
3. Cease physical activity when the temperature climbs above 88 degrees F unless the individual is trained and heat-acclimated.[9]

Heat stress is precipitated by imprudent exercise in a hot and humid environment, but many incidents occur when the temperature is mild and the humidity is high. The latter weather conditions are deceptive and the possibility of the occurrence of heat illness at these times must be recognized. Heat illness may be prevented by adhering to a few simple guidelines. Dehydration (loss of water) can be avoided by liberally drinking water (or a beverage which is low in sugar and salt) thirty to forty minutes prior to the workout, by drinking eight ounces every fifteen to twenty minutes during the workout, and by continuing to drink after the workout.

We do not voluntarily drink all that is needed to replace the fluid lost during exercise, so a good rule is to satisfy thirst and then drink some more. Research has shown that our thirst mechanism is not well attuned to our tissue needs and cannot be relied upon as a gauge for fluid replacement. The fluid we drink, preferably water, should be as cold as can be tolerated because it will absorb some of the body's heat as it is warmed to body temperature. There is no physiological data contradicting the use of cold water for the dual purpose of replacing fluid and lowering body temperature. A few people respond to cold water after exercise with nausea and headache. Should this occur it is advisable to drink slowly and/or drink tepid water.

Do not wear rubberized or plastic clothing while exercising because these garments promote sweating but retard its evaporation and seriously impede the cooling process. A supersaturated microenvironment is created between the skin and these garments which can lead very quickly to dehydration and heat illness.

Salt (sodium chloride) is lost in substantial quantities during the initial stages of the physical fitness program but as training continues, the body learns to conserve salt during exercise. This tends to increase its concentration in the body in relation to the fluid that remains while sweating is in progress. Taking salt during or after exercise is neither helpful nor desirable as it will interfere with the absorption of water from the gastrointestinal tract. The critical factor continues to be the replacement of water rather than salt.[10]

Available evidence shows conclusively that Americans eat too much salt. It is used as an additive in most processed foods so a deliberate attempt to ingest more seems unnecessary. Salt tablets are unacceptable as a method of salt replacement for the following reasons: 1) they are stomach irritants which may produce nausea and vomiting, 2) they may perforate the stomach lining; they sometimes pass through the body undissolved, 3) and they attract fluid to the gut from other tissues where it is needed and thereby enhance dehydration.

Potassium is also lost in sweat. Potassium and sodium are necessary for the contraction of muscles including the heart muscle. We have seen that deliberate salt replacement is not necessary. What about potassium replacement? Many authorities suggest that regular exercisers should eat some potassium rich foods daily such as citrus fruits and juices, potatoes, dates, bananas, and nuts. Bassler has shown that a number of deaths which occurred during the cool-down phase of exercise could be attributed to potassium depletion.[11] However, Costill reports that marathoners and ultramarathoners who did not season their food but ran fifteen to twenty-five miles per day did not develop electrolyte deficiencies.[10] Further, subjects who were given only thirty percent of their normal potassium consumption and were forced to dehydrate and lose seven to eight pounds of sweat per day for eight days showed no substantial changes in their electrolyte stores. Costill further contends that a single normal meal will replace the electrolytes lost during exercise. We might conclude that if one consumes a balanced diet and replaces the fluid lost during exercise, it probably is not necessary to make a special effort to replace salt and potassium.

Modifications in the exercise program should be considered during hot weather. Participants should schedule their workout during the cooler times of the day. Shady locations where water may be obtained should be used. Clothing should be light, loose, and porous in order to facilitate the evaporation of sweat. It is wise to slow the pace and/or shorten the distance on particularly oppressive days. Be especially alert for rapid weight loss because this may indicate an excessive loss of fluid. If you do not enjoy exercising in hot weather and cannot make the suggested schedule adjustments, try to move the program indoors into air conditioned comfort. The health benefits of exercise can be achieved there just as well. The important point is to continue to exercise to maintain what you have gained.

Jogging in Cold Weather

Problems related to exercise in cold weather include frostbite, hypothermia (abnormally low body temperature) and occasionally hyperthermia (abnormally high body temperature). The most frequently occurring cold-weather injury to young, healthy adults is frostbite, which can lead to permanent circulatory damage and possible loss of the frostbitten part due to gangrene. This can be prevented by adequately protecting susceptible areas such as fingers, toes, nose, ears, and facial skin. Gloves, preferably mittens, should be worn to protect the hands and fingers. A stocking or toboggan type hat should be worn because it can be pulled down to protect the ears and to prevent significant heat loss through the bare head by radiation due to the poor vasoconstriction responses (clamping down of blood vessels) in the scalp. In very cold environments, participants may use surgical masks, ski masks, and scarves to keep facial skin warm and to moisten and warm inhaled air. All exposed flesh is vulnerable to frostbite when the temperature is very low and the windchill factor is high. (See Table 2.1)

Hypothermia occurs when body heat is lost faster than it can be produced. Exposure to cold temperatures, pain, and wind chill combined with fatigue rob the body of heat. The body reacts with vasoconstriction of peripheral blood vessels as it attempts to conserve heat for the vital internal organs. Shivering, an involuntary contraction of the muscles, increases body heat. The shivering muscles produce no work so most of the expended energy appears as heat.

Surprisingly, hyperthermia may occur when one exercises in cold weather. Such cases occur when too much clothing is worn. This problem can be avoided by wearing several layers of light clothing that will trap warm insulating air between the layers.

TABLE 2.1 Wind Chill Index

Wind Speed in MPH	Actual Thermometer Reading (°F)											
	50	40	30	20	10	0	−10	−20	−30	−40	−50	−60
	Equivalent Temperature (°F)											
Calm	50	40	30	20	10	0	−10	−20	−30	−40	−50	−60
5	48	37	27	16	6	−5	−15	−26	−36	−47	−57	−68
10	40	28	16	4	−9	−21	−33	−46	−58	−70	−83	−95
15	36	22	9	−5	−18	−36	−45	−58	−72	−85	−99	−112
20	32	18	4	−10	−25	−39	−53	−67	−82	−96	−110	−124
25	30	16	0	−15	−29	−44	−59	−74	−88	−104	−118	−133
30	28	13	−2	−18	−33	−48	−63	−79	−94	−109	−125	−140
35	27	11	−4	−20	−35	−49	−67	−82	−98	−113	−129	−145
40[1]	26	10	−6	−21	−37	−53	−69	−85	−100	−116	−132	−148

LITTLE DANGER (for properly clothed person)	INCREASING DANGER — Cover up fully (hands, ears, face, head, etc.)	GREAT DANGER — Exercise Indoors

[1]Wind speeds greater than 40 MPH have little additional effect.
Adapted from Sharkey, B. J. *Physiology of Fitness*, Champaign, Ill: Human Kinetics Publishers, 1979, p. 226.

Dressing in this manner allows the participant to peel off a layer or two as the metabolic heat produced by exercise increases. The amount and type of clothing worn should allow for the evaporation of sweat and help achieve a balance between the amount of heat produced and the amount of heat lost. Clothing that becomes saturated with sweat is rapidly cooled and can quickly chill a participant who is working or exercising in cold weather.

Very often people may experience a hacking cough for a minute or two following exercise in cold weather. This is a normal response and should not cause alarm. Very cold dry air cannot be fully moistened when it is inhaled rapidly and in large volumes during exercise, so the lining of the throat dries out. When exercise is discontinued, the respiratory rate slows and the volume of incoming air decreases, allowing the body to fully moisturize it. The lining is remoistened and coughing stops.

Some people develop chest pain while exercising in cold weather and fear that the blood vessels in the chest are being constricted or that the lungs are becoming frostbitten. But inhaled air is adequately warmed before it reaches the lungs. Data on armed forces personnel who were marched for several hours in subzero temperatures showed no ill effects to lung tissue. There is no evidence to support the notion that lung tissue is subject to frostbite in cold weather. Those who experience chest pain upon exertion in the cold should consult a physician to determine if an organic or physiological problem exists. If a medical problem is identified, the physician's recommendations regarding exercise should be followed. If a problem is not identified but chest pain in cold weather persists, the workout should be moved indoors. This simple act may be all that is necessary to continue the program during the winter months.

COMMON SURFACES FOR JOGGING

Soft, level, grassy surfaces are best because there is less shock to the feet, legs, and hips. Public parks, golf courses, and playing fields fit the requirements nicely. Walk the course before jogging upon it. Familiarize yourself with the terrain, locate uneven surfaces, holes, jutting rocks, etc. If it does not pass inspection, forget it and locate another. Artificial surfaces, the kind found on some running tracks and football fields, are soft, resilient, level, and away from traffic. These are excellent surfaces for jogging. Dirt roads and cinder tracks are also fine. Dirt roads may be crowned, that is, higher in the middle than on the sides. Jogging on the side or slope of the road puts a different type of pressure on the feet and legs because the force of landing is distributed to the outside of one foot and to the inside of the other. The added and unaccustomed pressure on the joints could lead to injury so if traffic permits, try to jog on the crown which offers a more level surface.

City streets and sidewalks are the poorest surfaces for jogging because they are rigid and abrasive. The force of landing produces more comparative strain upon the body than the other surfaces. In addition, cement sidewalks are composed of surfaces which are similar to sandpaper and they produce accelerated shoe wear. Jogging on crowded city streets is a very risky business. Drivers are not always courteous so life and limb may be at stake. Secondly, carbon monoxide and other auto emissions are inimical to health as well as to jogging. Hard surfaces should be avoided entirely if at all possible during the early months of the program. After the muscles, ligaments, and tendons have been conditioned, the jogger can periodically run courses over hard surfaces. But orthopedic physicians unanimously agree that even long-time joggers cannot continually use these surfaces with impunity; eventually stress injuries will occur.

SUGGESTIONS FOR DEVELOPING A JOGGING PROGRAM

The prospective jogger's initial level of fitness will determine his or her entry point into the program. Level of fitness can be approximated with one of several field tests. The 1.5 mile Walk/Run Test and instructions on how to administer and interpret it appear in Appendix B. Bench stepping tests may also be employed but these yield less accurate results and will not be considered in this text. Treadmill and bicycle ergometer tests are not available to large numbers of people so they too will not be considered.

However, pre-testing with any of these instruments is not essential. A little common sense combined with an honest appraisal of one's past activity patterns would suggest the entry level for jogging. Adjustments in this level would result from trial and error attempts at pacing monitored by heart rate and perceived exertion blended with the principles and guidelines previously discussed. Some beginners may find that walking for several weeks will be a prerequisite for jogging. Others may begin by alternating walking with jogging to cover the desired distance until the distance can be traversed entirely by jogging. A few others may be fit enough to slow jog a given distance picking up the pace or increasing the distance as fitness improves.

Use the feedback from target zone heart rate as well as subjective feelings emanating from the body to sense when an increase in pace and/or duration is desirable and necessary. Duration takes precedence over intensity; intensity, however, should be in the target zone. When the workout is over, the jogger should feel pleasantly tired and relaxed. As stated by George Sheehan, noted philosopher, runner, and cardiologist, the key to success is: "train, don't strain."

You now have the information and knowledge to begin your jogging program. The remainder of this text will focus upon some of the major physiological and psychological benefits which can be expected to occur.

GOOD LUCK.

SUMMARY

Prospective joggers who have been sedentary should begin exercising gradually and progress slowly as fitness improves. The training effect will occur when the intensity, frequency, duration, overload and progression are within appropriate limits.

People of any age who exhibit one or more of the risk factors associated with heart disease should have a maximal exercise tolerance test which is monitored by a physician. Young people who are asymptomatic do not need an exercise tolerance test. Probably everyone forty-five years of age and older, regardless of their state of health, should have such a test whether or not they have been exercising because it may detect latent heart disease, it establishes a safe zone for exercise and the ECG can be used as a baseline with which to compare ECGs taken at later dates.

The principles of exercise should be manipulated to achieve exercise objectives. The clearer the objectives the greater the likelihood of achieving a match between them and the program to be followed. Jogging heart rate should be between sixty-five and ninety percent of the maximal heart rate for fifteen to sixty minutes for three to five days per week. Overload should be applied systematically and only when it is warranted.

Warm-up is necessary to prepare the musculoskeletal and cardiorespiratory systems for vigorous activity. By the same token, cool-down following exercise is equally as important. Static stretching should be employed during both phases.

Correct jogging form will result in greater mechanical efficiency as the jogger covers the ground and this in turn should reduce susceptibility to injury. It is important to commit some effort to improving jogging form.

The mechanisms of heat loss are conduction, radiation, convection and evaporation. Evaporation of sweat is the major means of ridding the body of heat during exercise. High humidity reduces the effectiveness of evaporation. If this is accompanied by high temperature, it will be difficult, if not impossible, to lose the heat generated from jogging. This type of weather necessitates a knowledge of the principles related to heat loss as well as adjustments in training routines in order to avoid heat stress.

It is not necessary for joggers to add salt to their diet. There is also evidence to indicate that potassium supplements or potassium rich diets are unnecessary. The important ingredient to closely monitor is fluid intake.

Frostbite is the most hazardous threat to joggers who exercise outdoors in cold weather. Layers of clothing and care in covering hands, ears, face and feet will usually prevent any problems.

Choose your jogging surfaces as carefully as you choose a pair of running shoes. Good shoes are a must and resilient surfaces will decrease the probability of injury.

REFERENCES

1. American College of Sports Medicine. *Guidelines For Exercise Testing and Prescription,* (3rd Edition), Philadelphia: Lea & Febiger, 1986.
2. Higdon, H. "If You Want Long Life — Exercise," *50 Plus,* 17, August, 1986.
3. Borg, G. A. V. "Perceived Exertion: A Note On History and Methods," *Medicine and Science in Sports,* 5:90, 1973.
4. Morgan, W. P. and Borg, G. A. V. "Perception of Effort and the Prescription of Physical Activity," *Mental Health and Emotional Aspects of Sports,* (T. Craig, ed), Chicago: American Medical Association, 1976.
5. Falls, H. B., Baylor, A. M., and Dishman, R. K. *Essentials of Fitness,* Philadelphia: Saunders College, 1980.
6. Moffatt, R. J. and others. "Placement of Tri-Weekly Training Sessions: Importance Regarding Enhancement of Aerobic Capacity," *Research Quarterly,* 48:583, 1977.
7. "American College of Sports Medicine Position Statement On the Recommended Quantity and Quality of Exercise for Developing and Maintaining Fitness in Healthy Adults," *Medicine and Science in Sports,* 10:No. 8, 3, 1978.
8. Barnard, R. J. and others. "Cardiovascular Responses to Sudden Strenuous Exercise — Heart Rate, Blood Pressure, and ECG," *Journal of Applied Physiology,* 34:833, 1973.
9. Sharkey, B. J. *Physiology of Fitness,* Champaign, Ill: Human Kinetics Publisher, Inc., 1984.
10. Costill, D. L. *Inside Running: Basics of Sports Physiology,* Indianapolis: Benchmark Press, 1986.
11. Bassler, T. J. "Deaths During the Cool Down Period," *American Medical Joggers Association Newsletter,* 7, March, 1984.

CHAPTER THREE

The Reduction Equation: Diet + Exercise = Weight Control

BASIC NUTRITION

Carbohydrates, fats, protein, vitamins, minerals and water are the basic nutrients, which when taken in proper amounts, allow the body to perform its many functions. They provide fuel for muscle contraction, maintain and repair body tissues, regulate chemical reactions at the cellular level, conduct nerve impulses, contribute to growth and reproduction, etc. It is the carbohydrates, fats, and proteins which supply the calories in the diet. Vitamins, minerals and water are acaloric.

Metabolism is the sum total of chemical reactions whereby the energy liberated from food is made available to the body. Two processes are involved: (1) anabolism — substances are built into new tissues or stored in some form for later use, and (2) catabolism — the breakdown of complex materials to simpler ones for the release of energy for muscular contraction.

Catabolism occurs when food is combined with oxygen. This process, referred to as oxidation, transforms food materials into heat or mechanical energy. The energy value of food is expressed as a calorie. In this text, we will deal with the large caloric (Kcal) which is the amount of heat needed to increase the temperature of one kilogram of water (slightly more than one quart) by one degree centigrade. This is sometimes referred to as the nutritionist's calorie in that it is the unit that is commonly used to assign the caloric value to food.

CARBOHYDRATES

Carbohydrates (CHO) are organic compounds composed of one or more sugars (saccharides) which are derived from plants. Carbohydrates consist of monosaccharides (simple sugar), disaccharides (combination of two simple sugars), and polysaccharides (the joining of three or more simple sugars to form starch and glycogen).

Table sugar, corn syrup, molasses, and honey are examples of simple sugars. Americans, active and inactive, consume too much of these substances — approximately 125 pounds per person per year. Most of this is in the form of hidden sugar; that is, it is included in processed foods. Canned soups and vegetables, canned meats, cereal, dairy products, soft drinks and many other items are laden with sugar. Simple sugars are called "empty calories" because they are rich in calories but provide little or no nutrition. Many authorities feel that the excessive consumption of simple sugars leads to obesity, diabetes, elevated cholesterol, heart disease and dental caries.

Starches, such as rice, potatoes, cereal grains and unprocessed fruits and vegetables are some of the complex carbohydrates. These supply energy, vitamins, minerals, fiber, and water. They are broken down through complex digestive processes to simple sugar for absorption by the body. One might conjecture that consuming simple sugars to begin with would save all of the intermediate steps needed to oxidize complex carbohydrates. The problem with this ostensibly logical position is that humans have not had enough time to adapt to the digestive demands of simple sugar. It's only in the last few decades that this category of food has become so available. When consumed, it gets into the blood stream rapidly and triggers an abnormal insulin response which causes large swings in blood sugar level. On the other hand, the complex carbohydrates are broken down slowly, get into the blood stream slowly, and the insulin response is more precise.

When oxidized, carbohydrates yield approximately four calories per gram. Because they are oxygen rich, they constitute our most efficient source of fuel. They are the major energy supplier in high intensity work of short duration and in exercise of a vigorous nature for up to sixty to ninety minutes.

Complex carbohydrates are low in fat and high in fiber, both of which can help protect against heart disease and certain types of cancer. The fiber in complex carbohydrates speeds up transit time of the contents in the digestive tract thereby shortening the time for the absorption of harmful products such as cholesterol. Low fiber diets are associated with colon cancer, colon polyps, hemorrhoids, diverticulitis and gall bladder disease.

Foods high in complex carbohydrates promote the storage of glycogen in the liver and muscles. Increasing the storage of glycogen enhances aerobic performance of long duration such as marathon running and long distance cycling.[1, 2] People who do not run such long distances should consume a diet rich in complex carbohydrates primarly because it is a healthy way to eat. Active adults should consume fifty to fify-five percent of their calories in the form of complex carbohydrates and an additional ten percent in the form of simple sugar.[3] People who train for and compete in prolonged endurance events should consume sixty-five to seventy percent of their calories from the carbohydrate group.

FATS

Fats are energy dense organic compounds that yield approximately 9.1 calories per gram. They have a relatively low oxygen content when compared to carbohydrates and consequently are not as efficient as sources of fuel. It takes more than twice the amount of oxygen to liberate energy from fat than from carbohydrates. But we store at least fifty times more energy in the form of fat than as carbohydrates.

Fats (lipids) consist of three major types: triglycerides, sterols, and phospholipids. The triglycerides are the most abundant type of fat, representing ninty-five percent of the fat that is eaten as well as that which is stored within the body. The sterols have a structure similar to cholesterol. The phospholipids are similar to a triglyceride except that one of the fatty acids is replaced by a phosphorous-containing acid. The triglycerides are composed of three fatty acids attached to a molecule of glycerol. Fatty acids are chains of carbon, oxygen, and hydrogen atoms which are classified as saturated or unsaturated, based upon their chemical structure. A fatty acid is saturated when all of its carbons are occupied with hydrogen and unsaturated when some carbon sites in the chain are free of hydrogen. Monosaturates are neutral fats with two points in the carbon chain that are free of hydrogen. Olive oil is an example. Polyunsaturated fatty acids have more than two points in the chain that are free of hydrogen. Most polyunsaturated fats are found in plants as a constituent of the protective coating of leaves and the skin of the seeds. Saturated fats come from animal flesh and dairy products, have a high melting point, and solidify at room temperature. Bacon grease is an example. Unsaturated fats come from vegetable sources, have a lower melting point, and remain liquid at room temperature. Corn oil is an example.

Polyunsaturated oils should be refrigerated to keep them from becoming rancid. They are vulnerable to spoilage when left to stand at room temperature because oxygen attacks those points in the chain that are unoccupied by hydrogen. To counteract spoilage the food industry adds hydrogen to some of the free bonds through the process of hydrogenation. The fat then loses its polyunsaturated characteristics as well as its health benefits.

Americans continue to consume forty to forty-five percent of their calories in the form of fat, half of which is saturated. Total fat should be reduced to twenty to thirty percent of the total calories, with most of the reduction coming from the saturated fats. The United States Senate Select Committtee On Nutrition and Human Needs recommended in 1977 that the number of calories in the diet coming from fat should be reduced to thirty percent of the total calories ingested.[4] Recently the American Heart Association[5] and the American Institute for Cancer Research[6] also recommended that fat in the diet be reduced to thirty percent of the total calories. Some authorities suggest that the total amount of fat in the diet can be reduced to even lower levels with no harmful effects. The body can synthesize its fat requirements from carbohydrates and protein. It is virtually impossible to eat a diet free of fat. Even vegetarian diets provide five to ten percent of their calories as fat. Only two fatty acids, linoleic acid and linolenic acid, are essential in that they cannot be synthesized by other substances in the body. They must be obtained in the diet but they are easily attained because they are widely distributed in meat, fish, poultry, vegetables and vegetable oils.

Reducing total fat in the diet to thirty percent is the first phase of the battle. The second involves the equal distribution of fat calories among the polyunsaturates, saturates and monosaturates, that is, about ten percent of the fat calories should come from each.[7]

Fat serves many vital functions: It is a significant energy source that provides up to seventy percent of the calories needed while the body is at rest. It is responsible for the storage, transport, and absorption of the fat soluble vitamins. It is an essential component of nerve fibers and cell walls. It protects vital organs from physical trauma by acting as a shock absorber, and finally it acts as an insulator against the loss of body heat. Excessive amounts of dietary or stored fat are not required to support these functions.

PROTEIN

Protein is one of the most misused and abused of the nutrients. It has been advertised as a high-energy food. In the Roman Empire, gladiators were fed large amounts of animal muscle tissue in the belief that this practice would build human muscle tissue. Many of today's body builders, weight lifters, and power lifters continue this practice. They consume enormous quantities of protein-rich foods and supplements in the belief that active people cannot obtain too much protein.

Protein is an essential nutrient that yields approximately 4.1 calories per gram but whose energy is liberated for the building and repair of body tissues; the formation of enzymes, hormones, antibodies and hemoglobin; the transportation of fats and other nutrients in the blood; the maintenance of acid-base balance in tissue fluids; and supplying energy for muscular work when there is a shortage of carbohydrates and fat.

Proteins are complex chemical structures containing carbon, oxygen, hydrogen, and nitrogen. These elements are combined into chains of different structures called amino acids. There is general agreement that the proteins of all living tissue consist of twenty different amino acids. Two other rare amino acids have been identified but they are found in very few proteins. Eight of the amino acids are essential because they cannot be manufactured in the body; these can only be obtained through the diet.

In order to build body tissues, all of the amino acids must be present simultaneously. This is analogous to building a house. Construction progresses unimpeded as long as all of the building materials are at the site, but if there is no mortar to lay the bricks, construction stops until it is supplied. Similarly, the building of body tissue progresses to completion when all of the amino acids (the body's building blocks) are present, but if one or more is missing construction stops at that point. Complete proteins, those containing all the amino acids, are found in meat, fish, poultry and dairy products. The proteins found in vegetables and cereal grains generally do not contain all of the amino acids but complementary foods from these two groups may be selected so that one supplies those amino acids missing in the other.

Legumes such as kidney and lima beans, black-eyed peas, garden peas, lentils, and soybeans are excellent sources of protein. Although their protein is not quite the caliber of that in meat they are rich in fiber, iron, and B-vitamins and they are low in fat.

Daily protein requirements vary according to our position in the life cycle. Infants require about 2.2 grams of protein per kilogram of body weight to support growth. Adolescents require 1.0 gram per kilogram and adults need 0.8 gram per kilogram. The typical American diet contains more than adequate amounts of protein. There seems to be no advantage in consuming more than fifteen percent of the total calories in the form of protein. Excessive intakes of protein — more than twenty percent of the total calories when the total calories are adequate — may possibly be hazardous. Protein overload has led to liver enlargement in animal subjects[8]; promotes calcium excretion in humans[9]; may raise serum cholesterol if a significant amount of protein comes from animal sources[10]; and crowds out important nutrient and fiber foods such as fruit, vegetables and grains from the diet.[9] Excessive protein can cause dehydration because extra water is needed to rid the body of unused or wasted nitrogen. This can be a significant problem for active people because of the additional fluid loss in the form of perspiration during a workout. Additionally, protein foods are expensive. Consuming greater amounts of protein does not enhance physical performance but that is not the function of protein.

VITAMINS

Vitamins are noncaloric organic compounds found in small quantities in most foods. All vitamins are either fat-soluble or water-soluble. The fat-soluble vitamins A, D, E, and K are stored in the liver and fatty tissues until they are needed. The water-soluble vitamins, C and the B complex group, are not stored for any appreciable length of time and must be replenished daily.

Vitamins function as coenzymes that promote the many chemical reactions that occur in the body around the clock.

Vitamin deficiencies result in a variety of diseases; therefore, an adequate daily intake is necessary for optimal health. The recommended daily allowances (RDA) have been established for most of the vitamins. These amounts are needed to prevent the occurrence of diseases that are the result of vitamin deficiencies, but they do not represent optimal values. Many people require larger quantities than the RDA. But an alarming trend — the practice of taking megadoses of vitamins in the mistaken belief that extremely large doses will prevent or cure anything — has surfaced in recent years.

Manufacturers and advertisers have convinced the public that the American diet is so deficient in vitamins that supplementation is a necessity. Those who supplement heavily may experience vitamin toxicity, particularly from overindulgence in the fat-soluble group. Too much Vitamin A results in gastrointestinal problems, nausea, joint pain, stunted growth, and enlargement of the liver and kidneys. An excess of Vitamin D may result in headache, nausea, diarrhea, and deposition of calcium in the soft tissues. Toxicity from megadoses of the water-soluble vitamins is less likely since excesses are excreted but some occurrences have been reported.

Synthetic vitamins in pill form seem to be as good and sometimes better than their "natural" counterparts in pill form although the manufacturers of the so called natural products would have us believe differently. The truth is that the body's cells cannot tell the difference between synthetic and natural vitamins. For instance, vitamin C in pill form made from rose hips would have to be as big as a marshmallow to come close to the minimum daily requirement. As a result, the manufacturers will add a significant amount of synthetic vitamin C, then label the product as "natural" and charge much more money for it.

Studies have shown that physical performance deteriorates when there is a vitamin deficiency. Energy output decreases, fatigue occurs more rapidly and muscle soreness occurs. These changes return to normal when vitamin intake is restored. Taking larger than needed amounts of vitamins does not result in increases in energy, strength or resistance to fatigue. Active people consume more vitamins than sedentary people because they take in more calories. People who are concerned about not getting enough vitamins through the diet, but unwilling to make appropriate dietary changes, can take a one-a-day brand. More than this amount is unnecessary and costly.

MINERALS

Minerals are inorganic substances that exist freely in nature. They are found in the earth's soil and water and they pervade some of its vegetation. Minerals maintain or regulate such physiological processes as muscle contractions, normal heart rhythm, body water supplies, acid-base balance of the blood, and nerve impulse conduction. Calcium, phosphorous, potassium, sulpher, sodium, chloride, and magnesium are the major minerals. These are classified as major because they occur in the body in quantities greater than five grams. The trace minerals or micronutrients number a dozen or more. The distinctions between the major and trace minerals is one of quantity rather than importance. Deficiencies of either can have serious consequences.

Sodium, potassium, and chloride are the primary minerals lost through perspiration. Sodium, the positive ion in sodium chloride (table salt), is one of the body's major electrolytes (ions that conduct electricity). Americans consume six to eighteen grams of sodium daily but only one to three grams is recommended.[11] About one-third of our salt consumption comes from table salt and one-quarter to one-half comes from processed foods.[12] Excessive salt intake is linked with hypertension. Sodium deficiency is rare in the U.S.

Joggers who exercise vigorously in hot weather are often concerned about replacing the salt which is lost in sweat and sometimes they make a special effort to restore the salt level. Conscious salt replacement is unnecessary since most Americans consume too much anyway. Salt depletion among active people is unlikely because they consume more than the average number of calories. Since salt is widely distributed in food, processed and otherwise, the increased caloric intake of active people compensates for that which is lost as a result of exercise.

Sodium is found in the fluid outside of the cells while potassium is found within cellular fluid. The temporary exchange of sodium and potassium across the cell's membrane permits the transmission of neural impulses and the contraction of muscles. Low potassium levels interfere with muscle cell nutrition and lead to muscle weakness and fatigue. Potassium is essential for the maintenance of the heart beat. Starvation and very low calorie diets for prolonged periods may produce sudden death from heart failure as potassium storage drops to critically low levels. Vomiting, diarrhea, and diuretics (medication to rid the body of excess water) reduce potassium levels. Chronic physical activity that produces heavy sweating may in time gradually diminish the potassium level in the body unless it is replaced periodically. This is easily accomplished because potassium is contained in many foods. It is particularly abundant in oranges, grapefruit, bananas, dates, nuts, fresh vegetables, meat and fish.

WATER

People may survive for a month or more without food but a few days without water will result in death. All body processes and chemical reactions take place in a liquid medium, therefore it is imperative to be fully hydrated and to make a special effort to replace water when it is lost. Under normal conditions adults drink 1.2 to 1.4 liters of fluid each day. More is needed when the weather is hot and humid or when one is physically active regardless of weather conditions.

Approximately forty to sixty percent of the body's weight consists of water. A sizable amount is stored in the muscles and some is stored in fat. By virtue of his larger muscle mass, the average male stores more water than the average female. Sixty-two percent of the total amount of water is found in the intracellular compartment (water which is within the cells), while the remaining thirty-eight percent is extracellular (water in the blood, lymph system, spinal cord fluid, saliva, etc.).

Water level in the body is maintained primarily by drinking fluids, but solid foods also contribute to water replenishment. Many foods — fruits, vegetables and meats — contain large amounts of water. Even seemingly dry foods such as bread and crackers contain some water. Solid foods add water in another way — they contribute metabolic water, which is one of the by-products of their breakdown to energy sources.

Most water loss occurs through urination, while small quantities are lost in the feces and in exhaled air from the lungs. Insensible perspiration (that which is not visible) accounts for a considerable amount of water loss. Exercise and hot humid weather increase sweating, so more water must be consumed during these times.

OVERWEIGHT — SCOPE OF THE PROBLEM

According to de Vries, "There are very few, very fat, very old people around. Your own observations — and the national statistics — clearly show that long life does not mean survival of the fattest."[13] Approximately eighty million Americans are overfat! According to the Department of Health and Human Services, the average male is eighteen pounds overweight and the average female is twenty-one pounds overweight. Paradoxically, Americans are getting fatter in spite of a five percent decrease in per-capita caloric consumption since 1910 and a national fitness boom since the late 1960s.[14]

When New York's Yankee Stadium was renovated a few years ago, its seating capacity was reduced by 9000 due to the increase in the width of the seats from nineteen to twenty-two inches to accommodate the growing American posterior.[15] A ten-state Midwestern study of young people ages eleven to eighteen showed that thirty-nine percent of the boys and thirty-three percent of the girls were overweight. An obese twelve year old has a twenty percent chance of becoming a normal weight adult; if still obese by age eighteen, the chances drop to less than five percent.[16] Approximately ten million of the nation's school children are over-weight.[17] Mayer has estimated that ten percent of America's school-age children are overweight or obese.[18] Additionally, fifteen percent of those under the age of thirty, fifteen to thirty percent of the adults, one-third of the elderly men, and one-half of the elderly women are obese. Of course all of these figures are estimates, implying some degree of error. Although the actual numbers may vary, the available data indicate that a significant number of Americans are overweight or obese and the trend is toward fatter rather than thinner. The latest figures came from a 14-member panel of physicians and nutritionists that estimated that thirty-four million American adults (approximately twenty percent of all people twenty years of age and older) are obese and that eleven million of these are categorized as being severely obese.[19] The typical American adult gains fifteen to twenty-five pounds between twenty-five and fifty years of age and most of them gain this weight gradually — less than a pound per year.[20] For most, this gain represents decreases in physical activity coupled with lowered energy requirements rather than an increase in caloric intake.

The terms "overweight" and "obesity" must be defined and differentiated. They are often used interchangeably or synonymously by the general public but in reality they differ considerably. Overweight refers to excessive body weight in relation to one's height, body build, and sex.[21] The determination of overweight is made by comparing a given individual's weight to a height-weight chart. These charts are meaningless because they do not consider body composition. As a result, two individuals may be classified as overweight but for entirely different morphological reasons. One may be overfat while the other may be very muscular. According to the charts, a 220 pound athlete may be overweight while carrying only twelve percent of his total body weight in the form of fat. This athlete is definitely not overfat. On the other hand, a sedentary 220 pounder of the same height may be carrying twenty-five percent of this weight in the form of fat. The latter individual is overweight because he is overfat; his body build or silhouette is considerably different from that of the athlete. A third individual may fall within the ideal weight range according to the charts while carrying twenty percent of that weight in the form of fat. Although this person is not overweight, he is decidedly overfat. Overweight is a nebulous and misleading term; it is important to assess the composition of body weight before any meaningful decisions are made regarding one's status. "Obesity" refers to overfat. It is a more specific term centering upon the percentage of the body weight composed of fat. Men are obese when twenty-three percent or more of their body weight is in the from of fat and women are obese when their fat content equals or exceeds thirty percent of their total weight.[22] Many authorities consider these two values to be too liberal and feel that obesity should be redefined at a lower percentage of body fat for each sex.

Overweight and obesity have complex physiological and psychological causes but the principles involved in weight loss are very simple. Energy cannot be destroyed; it is either used for work or converted into another form for storage. Individuals are in equilibrium when the calories consumed equal the calories used. Weight maintenance is lost when the equation is unbalanced in either direction. If the calories consumed exceed those that are used, the excess is converted to fat and stored. If the calories used exceed those that are consumed, weight will be lost because a portion of the stored fat must be mobilized to supply the extra need for fuel.

Scientifically, the principle is beautifully uncomplicated. We have made the process complex by inventing hundreds of ways to achieve weight loss painlessly and rapidly. Unfortunately, most of these methods are fruitless; some are actually dangerous and usually benefit only those who invent and promote them.

The preferred course of action is to prevent obesity from occurring rather than treating it after the fact. Evidence indicates that the seeds of obesity are planted very early in life, so early, in fact, that an affected individual has little say or control in the matter. Parental actions during this time may significantly influence the child's future weight problems. Early overfeeding may lead to the proliferation of fat cells. This is probably irreversible and will adversely affect efforts to control body weight during adulthood. There seems to be three critical periods when an increase in the number of fat cells may occur. These involve the last trimester of pregnancy, the first two years of postuterine life and adolescence (preadolescence for boys and all of adolescence for girls). The extra fat cells developed during these periods remain with us throughout life, adding to our storage capacity. Even during lean times these fat cells remain as empty pockets waiting to be filled. The increased number of fat cells complicates weight loss and maintenance because they exert some control over hunger. The concept of three critical periods in the generation of new fat cells is currently being challenged by some authorities who contend that fat cell number may increase at any time in life.[23]

Many overweight and obese people have normal numbers of fat cells. In these cases the existing fat cells hypertrophy (become larger). Compared to those with an abnormally high number of fat cells, these people may experience greater success in losing weight and maintaining the loss because they have a lesser number of fat cells to unload.

The message for parents is clear: Do not overfeed your children. If you do, you will be contributing to the probability of a life-long battle of weight control for your child.

OBESITY — A HEALTH HAZARD

The majority of Americans of all ages and both sexes can avoid obesity. It is a matter of choice, effort or lack of it, awareness of the hazards of obesity, and a commitment to do something about it. High-level wellness cannot be attained by the obese. Actuarial tables compiled by insurance companies indicate that fat people die younger than lean people. Individuals who are twenty percent overweight suffer early death at a rate fifty percent

higher than lean people, and those who are ten percent overweight have an early death rate that is one-third greater.[24]

Obesity is a major contributor to the development of Type II
(adult-onset) diabetes.[25] Fat people are at greater risk for coronary
artery disease, hypertension, post surgical complications,
gynecological abnormalities and elevation in blood lipids (cholesterol and triglycerides).[26] Extra fat in the thoracic (chest) area inter-
feres with breathing. Gout is more commonly found among the
obese. Obesity places a strain on the skeletal system and exacerbates lordosis, low back pain, and arthritis. Muscles and connective tissue in the abdominal wall overstretch and lose their elasticity, increasing the probability of abdominal hernias. Excessive fat
in the legs infiltrates the muscles, reducing their ability to contract
efficiently and seriously impeding the return of blood to the heart.
Blood collects in the leg veins, causing them to swell, harden and
become varicose.

In addition to these health hazards, the obese suffer from
economic and social discrimination, poor body image, and a
depressed self-concept. A survey of 1500 executives revealed that
body weight was inversely related to earning power. Only ten
percent of the executives in the upper income bracket were more
than ten pounds overweight, while forty percent of those in the
lower bracket were more than ten pounds overweight. Excessive
weight seems to be hazardous to purse and wallet. Fat people are
victims of discrimination because our culture is "slim" oriented.
We have become enamored with the thin silhouette. Advertise-
ments cater to the young and the slim. Clothing is made for thin
people and modeled by thin people. A recent Gallup Poll indicated that we are in the midst of a second fitness revolution.[27]
The first fitness movement was led by white middle and upper
class males. It began in the 1960s, when deaths due to cardiovascular disease were at their peak. The primary motivation for
exercise during this time was the enhancement of health. The
second movement is characterized by a tremendous influx of
women participants, it crosses socioeconomic lines, and, while
health enhancement still is the major motivator, many participants are seeking optimum development of their potential as
human beings.

Health enhancement remains the predominant reason for
participating in fitness activities but Americans are . . . "not just
pursuing exercise for its own sake, for the thinner look or a faster
running time. Instead they're lured onward by the belief that exer-

cise transforms their lives and helps them become the best humans they can be." Exercise is viewed as a tool for building a new self. The obese and overweight are the antithesis of this emerging spirit, thus establishing a climate for further discrimination. Fat people pay higher insurance premiums,[28] obese children are ridiculed by their slim peers, and military personnel are drummed out of service if they gain weight beyond an acceptable level.[29]

Fortunately obesity is reversible and so too are many of the risks with which it is associated. The preferred course of action would be to prevent obesity from occurring rather than trying to deal with it after the fact. This requires knowledgeable management of dietary and exercise habits both by individuals and their parents. Parents should teach and practice sound nutritional and exercise habits so that their children can proceed normally through periods in life when they are particularly vulnerable to fat cell proliferation.

EXERCISE BURNS CALORIES

A persistent misconception is that jogging, and other aerobic exercise, do not burn enough calories to make the effort worthwhile. Misinterpretation of caloric expenditure tables has contributed substantially to this misunderstanding. The tables show, for example, that to lose one pound, one must walk thirty-five miles, or chop wood for seven and one-half hours, or bike eleven hours, or play basketball for eight and one-half hours. The tables are essentially correct for the average size person but several errors are commonly made in their translation. First, the energy expenditures refer to fat tissue (3500 kcals per lb.) not to a pound of weight as measured with a scale. Scale weight includes the loss of liquid and muscles as well as fat while providing no clues to the relative losses of each. For this reason, the scale is a poor criterion to judge the success of weight loss. Second, these charts fail to fully account for the calories burned during recovery from exercise. The body does not turn off like a water tap when the workout is over. Instead, metabolism remains elevated for a period of time commensurate with the type and amount of exercise performed. It may extend for a few minutes following light exercise to as long as twenty-four hours following exhaustive exercise. The point is that the extra calories burned during the recovery period alone may result in a significant weight loss in a year's time. Third, one does not have to walk thirty-five miles in a single exercise session. The cumulative effect of exercise is what counts and this concept seems to be misunderstood by the general public. The calories expended in exercise today add to those which were expended yesterday and both will add to those expended tomorrow, and so on. Walking one extra mile per day will lead to the loss of one pound of fat in approximately thirty-five days for an average size male. This is a modest weight loss but it does add up to 10.5 pounds in a year. Two extra miles a day result in a twenty-one pound weight loss. This is a worthy accomplishment, particularly when one considers that excess weight accumulates slowly; we do not wake up one morning suddenly fat. We may perceive that it happened that way but the truth is that weight gain is insidious, taking months or years to occur. When we finally face the fact that the weight gained is beyond our acceptable limit, then we resolve to remove the excess as rapidly as possible. Impatient Americans, accustomed to instant tea, instant mashed potatoes, and instant rice also want instant weight loss and instant fitness. The laws of physiology and common sense dictate that this strategy is unsound and destined to fail. Success is dependent upon effort, time, and patience.

Jogging contributes significantly to weight loss. According to the American College of Sports Medicine, aerobic exercises that use 300 to 500 Kcals per bout will promote weight loss and a favorable change in body composition (the percent of fat to lean tissue). This translates to jogging three to five miles per workout based upon the generalization that an average size person expends 100 Kcals per mile. Actually the caloric cost per mile is based upon body weight rather than speed. Jogging is a weight bearing activity so it costs more to transport a larger body for a given distance than a smaller body. Study the values in Table A.1. in Appendix A. You will note that a 150 pound person expends 97 calories jogging a seven minute mile and 91 calories jogging a ten minute mile. The difference in energy expended is just six calories but the difference in effort is considerable. Notice also that a 210 pound person burns 130 calories jogging a nine minute mile while a 130 pounder burns only 80 calories at the same speed for a whopping 50 calorie difference. Body size makes a difference. The overweight person will expend more calories in the initial stages of the jogging program. The expenditure per mile will decline as weight is being lost but the participant will compensate by jogging further as fitness is gained. Increasing the distance rather than the intensity is the proper prescription for

meeting the objective of weight loss. The values in the chart apply
to both males and females.

EXERCISE AND APPETITE: EAT MORE. WEIGH LESS

To the uninitiated, the title of this section must seem at least
paradoxical if not impossible. How can one eat more and weigh
less? It sounds like a bit of alchemy or a get-rich-quick sales pitch.
But wouldn't it be nice to "have your cake and eat it too" —
without gaining weight? This is especially intriguing since it is
known that Americans are eating less and getting fatter. Since
weight gain and loss are a combination of calories consumed and
calories expended, it is obvious that the reduction in caloric consumption has been accompanied by a greater reduction in calories
expended. This explains our continued weight gain.

The results of animal and human studies during the last
thirty-five years have been equivocal and confusing regarding the
effect of exercise on appetite. The data have shown that exercise
may decrease, increase, or have no effect upon food intake. Just
a few short years ago, the scientific community adopted the position that one hour of mild to moderate exercise would exert an
anorexigenic effect (reduction in appetite).[30] The theory was that
food intake would decrease during the early days of exercise as
one was making the transition from inactivity to moderate exercise and persist until the level of exercise increased to above moderate levels. At this point the appetite would increase to be in
balance with energy expenditure. Other researchers tested these
assumptions but were unable to produce similar results. Exercise
did not seem to suppress the appetite except temporarily immediately after exercise. Most studies indicated that people either
continued to eat the same amount or increased their food intake
when they began exercising and were allowed to eat freely. Wood
investigated the effects of a year of jogging on previously sedentary middle-aged males.[31] The subjects were encouraged not to
reduce their food intake or to attempt to lose weight during the
course of the study. At the end of one year the men who ran the
most miles lost the most fat; secondly, the more miles the men
ran the more they increased their food intake; and thirdly, the
more fat the men lost, the more they increased their food intake.

Two studies at St. Luke's Hospital in New York showed that
the effect of exercise on the appetite is regulated to some extent
by the degree of obesity at the start of the program. Fifty-seven

days of moderate treadmill exercise resulted in a fifteen pound weight loss by obese female subjects. Their caloric intake during exercise compared to the preexercise period was essentially unchanged. This study was repeated with women who were close to "ideal weight" according to insurance company charts; the results were very different. Moderate treadmill exercise produced an immediate surge in appetite and these women maintained their "ideal body" weight.

Weight loss attempts in the U.S. have emphasized dietary restriction with continued sedentary living. This combination has led to consistent failure. Weight loss with this method is temporary and the majority of these weight watchers lose and gain weight many times during their lives. The eating patterns established during the diet period are short-lived. "Dieting actually makes the fat person even more unlike the slim person; he or she is simply a fat person reluctantly eating less, and the transformation into a true slim person has not occurred. It is not at all surprising, then, that the eat-less approach to weight loss and permanent weight control has not worked.[21] Each failure stimulates a rebound effect. The dieter regains the lost weight plus a few more pounds and each new attempt at weight loss produces more frustration and requires a more stringent diet.

Just how successful are weight loss programs that rely solely upon manipulation of dietary intake? The statistics are dismal. The U.S. Department of Public Health has estimated that only five percent of all dieters are successful in reducing to a target weight and maintaining the loss for one year. Further, only two percent are successful in achieving permanent weight loss.

A widely held assumption is that the obese eat substantially more than thin people. The evidence indicates that they eat less than normal-weight individuals who participate in light to moderate physical acivity.[20] Obese girls who were observed during summer camp ate less and were less active than normal-weight girls.[32] Similar results were obtained from observations of boys at summer camp.[33] Studies of obese adults have shown that the inception of their weight gain could be traced back to a time when a decrease in physical activity, rather than an increase in appetite, occurred. This pattern is evident through observation of people who are attempting to fit into and establish a career after college. The attention and time devoted to physical activity decreases but their appetites do not. Six to twelve months after graduation they are five to fifteen pounds heavier.

JOGGING STIMULATES METABOLISM

The resting metabolic rate (RMR) refers to the amount of energy required to sustain life while in the resting state. The RMR is measured in calories and pertains to the energy required to maintain body temperature and cellular metabolism. It is affected by age, sex, secretions from endocrine glands, nutritional status, sleep, fever, climate, body surface area, and muscle tissue. Principally due to less muscle tissue, the RMR of females is five to ten percent lower than males and fifteen percent lower than that of very muscular males.

In the past, the decline in RMR was presumed to be a natural aspect of aging. But age per se has relatively little effect. It seems that the acquired changes accompanying aging are primarily responsible for the decline in RMR. de Vries stated that ". . . it has been shown that the loss in human muscle tissue with age can entirely account for the downward trend in basal metabolism."[34] Muscle tissue uses more energy than fat during rest/or physical activity. Authorities estimate that we lose three to five percent of our active protoplasm from the protein containing organs (mostly from muscle tissue) each decade after twenty-five years of age. This loss is directly attributed to physical inactivity as we age and results in the all-too-common negative changes that are seen in body composition. Young and middle-aged subjects who were within plus or minus five percent of their ideal weight as determined by height, weight, and frame size charts illustrated the body compositon changes that occur with age.[35] Although both groups were within the ideal range for weight, the middle-aged subjects had twice as much body fat as the young subjects. These data show quite well that lost muscle weight that is replaced by a gain in fat weight produces negative changes in body composition even in the absence of weight gain.

Fat is less dense than muscle so it occupies more room in the body; hence the change in the configuration of the body. Table 3.1 illustrates some of the changes in body composition that occur as Americans age. The examples are hypothetical but they are based upon fact. The lean tissue values in the table apply to males, but the same trend is evident to a lesser degree in females because they have less lean tissue to lose.

Subject 1 typifies the inactive person who maintains his body weight while aging but experiences a change in body composition. The bathroom scale provides no clues regarding the change

TABLE 3.1   Effects of Physical Inactivity on Body Composition

Subject	Body Weight at age 20	Body Weight at age 60	Activity Level	Lean Tissue	Fat	Body Composition
1	150 lbs.	150	Inactive	Lost 12-20%	Gain	Changed
2	150 lbs.	135	Inactive	Lost 12-20%	No Gain	Changed
3	150 lbs.	165	Inactive	Lost 12-20%	Gain	Changed
4	150 lbs.	150	Active	No Loss	No Gain	Unchanged

but the mirror and fit of his clothes do. He must hold a tight reign on appetite because his resting caloric requirements have diminished. Subject 2 is inactive and chooses to lose weight with age to keep from becoming fatter — rare in our society. He loses one-quarter to one-half pound per year after age 30. This individual lost muscle tissue but has reduced his body weight. His body compositon has changed as a result — he is smaller all over. Due to the decline in metabolism from the loss of muscle, along with a lower body weight which diminishes the caloric cost of any weight-bearing movement, this individual must eat progressively less as the years pass to prevent a gain in fat tissue. Hunger would be a constant companion with this strategy. Subject 3 is probably most representative of the typical American who gains both fat and weight with age. Subject 4 is physically active throughout life. There is little muscle loss and no gain in fat weight. Many examples of this modern-day phenomenon continue to jog, cycle, swim, etc. Programs that build and maintain muscle tissue preserve the RMR and perpetuate a youthful body composition.

The energy used to sustain the RMR constitutes about sixty-five percent of the total number of daily calories expended by the average adult.[5] Then, from the perspective of weight control, it is important to preserve and/or enhance the metabolic rate and to do nothing to reduce it. Exercise fits the bill very nicely.

Metabolism is adversely affected by calorie restriction. In its quest of homostasis (the tendency to maintain a constancy of internal conditions) the body adapts to the reduced calorie intake by lowering the metabolic rate. This effort to economize in response to less food intake is a survival mechanism that protects people during lean times. Because the body learns to get by with less, the difference between calories eaten and calories needed narrows. This defense mechanism makes it possible for prisoners of war to survive internment in concentration camps. This same defense mechanism is operative in individuals who voluntarily reduce their food intake with the same result; a drop in RMR. As the RMR decreases, so too does the effectiveness of dieting. Regular vigorous exercise has the opposite effect: it accelerates the metabolic processes and increases body temperature during and after physical activity. The RMR may remain elevated for some time after exercise and probably contributes to more calories used as a result than had been previously thought. Under exercise conditions, the body is spending rather than hording calories.

Dieting reduces basal heat production. In one study, the basal heat of dieting obese students dropped to ninety-one percent of prediet levels in two weeks on a 500 calorie per day diet.[36] After the initial two weeks they switched to twenty to thirty minutes of exercise at sixty percent of their aerobic capacity. Basal heat production increased to normal values in three to four days and continued to increase for the next two weeks to a value equal to 107 percent of the prediet level. Meanwhile, the basal heat production of sedentary controls on a 500 calorie per day diet for the four weeks dropped to eighty-one percent of their prediet levels. This drop in heat production or energy expenditure partially explains why the actual weight lost by dieting is often less than the predicted weight loss. Zuti and Golding investigated the relationship between exercise, diet, and weight loss.[37] They analyzed the effects of three different strategies upon the quantity and quality of weight loss. Each strategy was designed to elicit a loss of one pound per week. The subjects were overweight women twenty-five to forty-five years of age. A summary of the results of the study appears in Table 3.2.

TABLE 3.2	Average Weight Lost By Groups

Weight Loss Strategy	Fat Tissue Loss (lbs.)	Lean Tissue Change (lbs.)	Total Weight Loss (lbs.)
Diet Only	−9.3	−2.4	−11.7
Exercise Only	−12.6	+ 2.0	−10.6
Diet and Exercise	−13.0	+ 1.0	−12.0

The "Diet Only" group reduced food intake by 500 calories per day and did not exercise. The "Exercise Only" group did not diet; instead, they increased their physical activity by 500 calories per day. The "Diet and Exercise" group reduced their caloric intake by 250 calories per day while increasing their caloric expenditure by the same amount. The aim of all three strategies was to lose one pound per week (500 cals/day × 7 days = 3500 cals.) and this objective was essentially accomplished. But the significant outcome of the study was that twenty-one percent of the total loss experienced by the "Diet Only" group was in the form of lean tissue. This occurred despite a nutritionally sound diet of modest calorie restriction. The other two groups lost fat (the true goal of weight loss programs) and gained rather than lost lean tissue.

More restrictive diets produce greater losses of lean tissue. Fasting or starvation results in substantial losses of lean tissue. The brain and central nervous system require glucose (sugar) as their only source of fuel. Glucose is produced from the breakdown of dietary carbohydrates, but fasting or starvation means zero nutrient intake. Under these circumstances, the body's protein from muscles, liver, and other organs is converted to glucose for the brain and central nervous system. Ninety percent of the body's glucose is formed in this manner and the other ten percent comes from glycerol (fat). The conversion of protein to glucose is a wasteful process because only half of the amino acids (the structure of protein) are used, while the other half must be removed. Ninety-five percent of all fat cannot be converted to glucose. The body adapts to fat as a major supplier of fuel by converting fatty acids to ketone bodies. Ketone bodies are organic acids that disturb the acid-base balance of the blood. They are the product of the incomplete breakdown of fat when carbohydrates are not available. The brain and central nervous system partially adapt and receive fifty percent of their fuel from ketones. The other fifty percent continues to come from the breakdown of the body's protein. Consequently, the RMR decreases significantly during the time of deprivation as the body attempts to conserve its lean tissue and fat stores. As the protein-containing organs progressively shrink, they perform less and less metabolic work and reduce the body's energy needs. The slowed-down metabolic engine results in less fat loss while body weight continues to fall rapidly. Concurrently, ketone bodies accumulate in the blood because they are produced in quantities that outstrip the body's ability to use or excrete them. The increase in blood acid level is potentially dangerous. Starvation should be avoided except for the extremely obese and then only under hospitalized medical supervision.

JOGGING AND THE UNDERWEIGHT

The focus thus far has been on weight loss rather than weight gain, but the purposeful gain of weight represents a real problem for the underweight. What constitutes underweight? This question has not been satisfactorily answered. Actuarial statistics indicate that those who are significantly below the average in body weight have a higher expected mortality rate. Marked underweight may be indicative of underlying disease and is as much of a risk for early death as obesity.

Being underweight may pose as much of a cosmetic problem for an affected individual as obesity is for an obese individual. An effective weight gain program should include regular resistance exercise in conjunction with five or six nutritious meals per day. High fat and sugary foods should be avoided because they are as unhealthy for the underweight as well as anyone else. Despite Herculean efforts, many underweight people find it as difficult to gain a pound as it is for the obese to lose one.

The amount and type of weight gain should be closely monitored. It is desirable to gain muscle tissue without increasing fat stores. Overeating without exercise will not accomplish this objective and it will not enhance physical appearance. In some extreme cases such as anorexia nervosa, where fat stores fall well below desirable levels, it is advisable to gain fat as well as muscle. Anorexics differ from other very thin people in their dietary habits. They voluntarily starve themselves and when they do eat, they induce vomiting to rid themselves of the calories. Laxatives are also part of the anorexic's repertoire. This condition requires medical and possibly psychiatric treatment. If treatment is not sought, or if it is unsuccessful, brain damage or death may ensue.

How thin is too thin? There are no hard and fast answers. The height-weight charts provide some clues. Individuals who are well below average for their height and frame size are underweight. They may be undermuscled or underfat or both. A better criterion concerns the percentage of total weight composed of fat. Healthy males who have more than five percent body fat are not endangering those biological functions that require fat. However, such males may not be satisfied with their very slim appearance. Females should not reduce their fat stores to levels that disturb the menstrual cycle. For college-age women, seventeen to eighteen percent body fat presents a slim, trim appearance with enough fat for the reproductive system to function in a normal manner.

DETERMINING PERCENT BODY FAT

There are a variety of ways to assess body fat ranging from using the subjective eyeball technique by standing naked in front of a mirror to the more scientific method of removing the fat from a cadaver. We will discuss some selected methods which fall somewhere between these two extremes.

Trying to determine body fat from standard height-weight charts is futile. The charts display desirable weights which have been compiled by insurance companies and reflect weights associated with low mortality rates. But these reveal nothing regarding percent body fat and they may be misleading. A very muscular individual may appear to be overweight by these charts. Overweight is not the issue, overfat is. An overfat person with less than average muscle may be in the desirable weight range.

Another problem associated with height-weight charts is the accuracy of the judgment that individuals must make regarding their frame size. A method of estimating frame size for those who wish to know it and for those who would like to use the height-weight charts for reasons of curiosity follows. Use a flexible tape measure and measure the circumference of the ankle at the smallest point above the two laterally protruding bones. Interpret the results as follows: for males small frame (less than 8"), medium frame (8-9½"), large frame (more than 9½"); for females small frame (less than 7½"), medium frame (7½-8¾"), and large frame (more than 8¾").

To use the height-weight charts, first calculate ankle size as described above in order to find frame size and then enter Table 3.3 under your sex, frame size and height. These are not the new tables which have been developed by Metropolitan Life because the new ones have been criticized for liberalizing the ideal weights and this author agrees with that opinion.

Hydrostatic weighing is unavailable for the general population. This method requires special equipment and a skilled technician. It involves weighing the subject while he/she is immersed

TABLE 3.3   Desirable Weights for Men and Women*

Men of Ages 25 and Over
Weight in Pounds According to Frame (In Indoor Clothing)

Height (with shoes on) 1-inch heels Feet Inches		Small Frame	Medium Frame	Large Frame
5	2	112-120	118-129	126-141
5	3	115-123	121-133	129-144
5	4	118-126	124-136	132-148
5	5	121-129	127-139	135-152
5	6	124-133	130-143	138-156
5	7	128-137	134-147	142-161
5	8	132-141	138-152	147-166
5	9	136-145	142-156	151-170
5	10	140-150	146-160	155-174
5	11	144-154	150-165	159-179
6	0	148-158	154-170	164-184
6	1	152-162	158-175	168-189
6	2	150-167	162-180	173-194
6	3	160-171	167-185	178-199
6	4	164-175	172-190	182-204

Women of Ages 25 and Over
For girls between 18 and 25, subtract 1 pound for each year under 25.

(with shoes on) 2-inch heels				
4	10	92- 98	96-107	104-119
4	11	94-101	98-110	106-122
5	0	96-104	101-113	109-125
5	1	99-107	104-116	112-128
5	2	102-110	107-119	115-131
5	3	105-113	110-122	118-134
5	4	108-116	113-126	121-138
5	5	111-119	116-130	125-142
5	6	114-123	120-135	129-146
5	7	118-127	124-139	133-150
5	8	122-131	128-143	137-154
5	9	126-135	132-147	141-158
5	10	130-140	136-151	145-163
5	11	134-144	140-155	149-168
6	0	138-148	144-159	153-173

*Courtesy of Metropolitan Life Insurance Company. Note: Weights given are for persons wearing indoor clothing and shoes. For nude weights, women should subtract from 2 to 4 lbs., and men from 5 to 7 lbs.

in water. One could then measure either the weight of the water displaced by the body or the weight of the body when completely submerged. When these data are plugged into appropriate formulas, the percent body fat may be ascertained. This is an accurate method.

Skinfold measurement is becoming more commonplace since several low cost calipers have made their way into the marketplace. In skilled hands, some of them correlate quite well (.90) with the more expensive brands found in most exercise physiology labs. The rationale for this technique is based on the fact that approximately fifty percent of the body's fat is located directly beneath the skin, therefore the skinfold, which is a double layer of skin and the underlying fat, may be measured with a caliper. In this text, the Jackson and Pollock generalized tables for age and sex are used to convert skinfold measurements (in millimeters) to percent fat. See Tables 3.4 and 3.5. The sites to enter the tables and the techniques for their measurement are presented in Figures 3.1 through 3.5.

SPOT REDUCTION

Spot reduction implies that one can reduce the fat content of a particular body part by doing specific exercises related to that part. Sit-ups and leg-lifts have been commonly used to reduce abdominal fat and waist girth while leaving the remainder of the body intact. The attractiveness of this concept has led an unsuspecting public to believe that with a little effort we can sculpt our bodies to suit our fancies. Spot reduction is a myth which is promoted by charlatans or unknowledgeable people who have a gimmick, gadget or system to sell which is supposedly designed to achieve fat reduction in localized areas of the body. The truth is that the buyer will probably reduce nothing but the size of his/her bank account. Localized exercise produces muscle tone and strength but it does not decrease the amount of fat at a given site. It will tighten up localized areas which may result in a difference in girth. For example, sit-ups done over a period of time will strengthen and firm the abdominals which will improve their ability to hold back the viscera. In this respect, waist girth or circumference may be decreased but fat content will remain unchanged. In order to reduce the fat stored in the stomach, back of the arms, buttock, or thighs, etc., the person must expend more calories than those which are consumed. As a result, fat will be lost from

TABLE 3.4   Percent Fat Estimates For Men*

Sum of Skinfolds (mm)	Age to the Last Year								
	Under 22	23 to 27	28 to 32	33 to 37	38 to 42	43 to 47	48 to 52	53 to 57	Over 58
8- 10	1.3	1.8	2.3	2.9	3.4	3.9	4.5	5.0	5.5
11- 13	2.2	2.8	3.3	3.9	4.4	4.9	5.5	6.0	6.5
14- 16	3.2	3.8	4.3	4.8	5.4	5.9	6.4	7.0	7.5
17- 19	4.2	4.7	5.3	5.8	6.3	6.9	7.4	8.0	8.5
20- 22	5.1	5.7	6.2	6.8	7.3	7.9	8.4	8.9	9.5
23- 25	6.1	6.6	7.2	7.7	8.3	8.8	9.4	9.9	10.5
26- 28	7.0	7.6	8.1	8.7	9.2	9.8	10.3	10.9	11.4
29- 31	8.0	8.5	9.1	9.6	10.2	10.7	11.3	11.8	12.4
32- 34	8.9	9.4	10.0	10.5	11.5	11.6	12.2	12.8	13.3
35- 37	9.8	10.4	10.9	11.5	12.0	12.6	13.1	13.7	14.3
38- 40	10.7	11.3	11.8	12.4	12.9	13.5	14.1	14.6	15.2
41- 43	11.6	12.2	12.7	13.3	13.8	14.4	15.0	15.5	16.1
44- 46	12.5	13.1	13.6	14.2	14.7	15.3	15.9	16.4	17.0
47- 49	13.4	13.9	14.5	15.1	15.6	16.2	16.8	17.3	17.9
50- 52	14.3	14.8	15.4	15.9	16.5	17.1	17.6	18.2	18.8
53- 55	15.1	15.7	16.2	16.8	17.4	17.9	18.5	18.1	19.7
56- 58	16.0	16.5	17.1	17.7	18.2	18.8	19.4	20.0	20.5
59- 61	16.9	17.4	17.9	18.5	19.1	19.7	20.2	20.8	21.4
62- 64	17.6	18.2	18.8	19.4	19.9	20.5	21.1	21.7	22.2
65- 67	18.5	19.0	19.6	20.2	20.8	21.3	21.9	22.5	23.1
68- 70	19.3	19.9	20.4	21.0	21.6	22.2	22.7	23.3	23.9
71- 73	20.1	20.7	21.2	21.8	22.4	23.0	23.6	24.1	24.7
74- 76	20.9	21.5	22.0	22.6	23.2	23.8	24.4	25.0	25.5
77- 79	21.7	22.2	22.8	23.4	24.0	24.6	25.2	25.8	26.3
80- 82	22.4	23.0	23.6	24.2	24.8	25.4	25.9	26.5	27.1
83- 85	23.2	23.8	24.4	25.0	25.5	26.1	26.7	27.3	27.9
86- 88	24.0	24.5	25.1	25.7	26.3	26.9	27.5	28.1	28.7
89- 91	24.7	25.3	25.9	26.5	27.1	27.6	28.2	28.8	29.4
92- 94	25.4	26.0	26.6	27.2	27.8	28.4	29.0	29.6	30.2
95- 97	26.1	26.7	27.3	27.9	28.5	29.1	29.7	30.3	30.9
98-100	26.9	27.4	28.0	28.6	29.2	29.8	30.4	31.0	31.6
101-103	27.5	28.1	28.7	29.3	29.9	30.5	31.1	31.7	32.3
104-106	28.2	28.8	29.4	30.0	30.6	31.2	31.8	32.4	33.0
107-109	28.9	29.5	30.1	30.7	31.3	31.9	32.5	33.1	33.7
110-112	29.6	30.2	30.8	31.4	32.0	32.6	33.2	33.8	34.4
113-115	30.2	30.8	31.4	32.0	32.6	33.2	33.8	34.5	35.1
116-118	30.9	31.5	32.1	32.7	33.3	33.9	34.5	35.1	35.7
119-121	31.5	32.1	32.7	33.3	33.9	34.5	35.1	35.7	36.4
122-124	32.1	32.7	33.3	33.9	34.5	35.1	35.8	36.4	37.0
125-127	32.7	33.3	33.9	34.5	35.1	35.8	36.4	37.0	37.6

*Sum of chest, abdominal, and thigh skinfolds. From Jackson, A.S. and M. Pollock. "Generalized Equations for Predicting Body Density of Men," *British Journal of Nutrition,* 49:497-504, 1978.

TABLE 3.5   Percent Fat Estimates For Women*

Sum of Skinfolds (mm)	Under 22	23 to 27	28 to 32	33 to 37	38 to 42	43 to 47	48 to 52	53 to 57	Over 58
				Age to the Last Year					
23- 25	9.7	9.9	10.2	10.4	10.7	10.9	11.2	11.4	11.7
26- 28	11.0	11.2	11.5	11.7	12.0	12.3	12.5	12.7	13.0
29- 31	12.3	12.5	12.8	13.0	13.3	13.5	13.8	14.0	14.3
32- 34	13.6	13.8	14.0	14.3	14.5	14.8	15.0	15.3	15.5
35- 37	14.8	15.0	15.3	15.5	15.8	16.0	16.3	16.5	16.8
38- 40	16.0	16.3	16.5	16.7	17.0	17.2	17.5	17.7	18.0
41- 43	17.2	17.4	17.7	17.9	18.2	18.4	18.7	18.9	19.2
44- 46	18.3	18.6	18.8	19.1	19.3	19.6	19.8	20.1	20.3
47- 49	19.5	19.7	20.0	20.2	20.5	20.7	21.0	21.2	21.5
50- 52	20.6	20.8	21.1	21.3	21.6	21.8	22.1	22.3	22.6
53- 55	21.7	21.9	22.1	22.4	22.6	22.9	23.1	23.4	23.6
56- 58	22.7	23.0	23.2	23.4	23.7	23.9	24.2	24.4	24.7
59- 61	23.7	24.0	24.2	24.5	24.7	25.0	25.2	25.5	25.7
62- 64	24.7	25.0	25.2	25.5	25.7	26.0	26.2	26.4	26.7
65- 67	25.7	25.9	26.2	26.4	26.7	26.9	27.2	27.4	27.7
68- 70	26.6	26.9	27.1	27.4	27.6	27.9	28.1	28.4	28.6
71- 73	27.5	27.8	28.0	28.3	28.5	28.8	29.0	29.3	29.5
74- 76	28.4	28.7	28.9	29.2	29.4	29.7	29.9	30.2	30.4
77- 79	29.3	29.5	29.8	30.0	30.3	30.5	30.8	31.0	31.3
80- 82	30.1	30.4	30.6	30.9	31.1	31.4	31.6	31.9	32.1
83- 85	30.9	31.2	31.4	31.7	31.9	32.2	32.4	32.7	32.9
86- 88	31.7	32.0	32.2	32.5	32.7	32.9	33.2	33.4	33.7
89- 91	32.5	32.7	33.0	33.2	33.5	33.7	33.9	34.2	34.4
92- 94	33.2	33.4	33.7	33.9	34.2	34.4	34.7	34.9	35.2
95- 97	33.9	34.1	34.4	34.6	34.9	35.1	35.4	35.6	35.9
98-100	34.6	34.8	35.1	35.3	35.5	35.8	36.0	36.3	36.5
101-103	35.3	35.4	35.7	35.9	36.2	36.4	36.7	36.9	37.2
104-106	35.8	36.1	36.3	36.6	36.8	37.1	37.3	37.5	37.8
107-109	36.4	36.7	36.9	37.1	37.4	37.6	37.9	38.1	38.4
110-112	37.0	37.2	37.5	37.7	38.0	38.2	38.5	38.7	38.9
113-115	37.5	37.8	38.0	38.2	38.5	38.7	39.0	39.2	39.5
116-118	38.0	38.3	38.5	38.8	39.0	39.3	39.5	39.7	40.0
119-121	38.5	38.7	39.0	39.2	39.5	39.7	40.0	40.2	40.5
122-124	39.0	39.2	39.4	39.7	39.9	40.2	40.4	40.7	40.9
125-127	39.4	39.6	39.9	40.0	40.4	40.6	40.9	41.1	41.4
128-130	39.8	40.0	40.3	40.5	40.8	41.0	41.3	41.5	41.8

*Sum of triceps, suprailium, and thigh skinfolds. From Jackson, A.S., M. Pollock, and A. Ward. "Generalized Equations for Predicting Body Density of Women," *Medicine and Science in Sports,* 12:175-182, 1980.

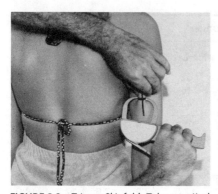

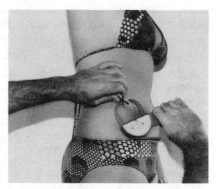

FIGURE 3.2 Triceps Skinfold. Take a vertical fold on the midline of the upper arm over the triceps halfway between the acromion and olecranon processes (tip of shoulder to tip of elbow). The arm should be extended and relaxed when the measurement is taken.

FIGURE 3.3 Suprailium Skinfold. Take a diagonal fold above the crest of the ilium directly below the mid-axilla (armpit).

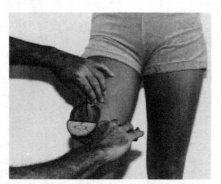

FIGURE 3.4 Thigh Skinfold. Take a vertical fold on the front of the thigh midway between the hip and knee joint.

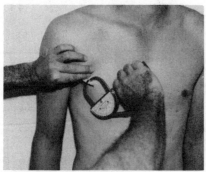

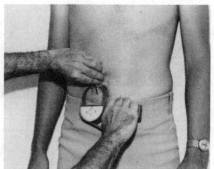

FIGURE 3.5 Chest Skinfold. Take a diagonal fold one-half of the distance between the anterior axillary line and nipple.

FIGURE 3.6 Abdominal Skinfold. Take a vertical fold about 3/8 inch from the navel.

all storage depots, including the site in question. If spot reduction were a reality, people with fat faces could chew gum everyday and eventually become people with thin faces. It just doesn't work.

SUMMARY

A significant number of Americans of all ages and both sexes are experiencing a weight problem. Most rely on dieting to lose excess weight but the overwhelming majority fail. Dieting will produce weight loss but at the cost of losing muscle tissue and a reduction in the metabolic rate. The result is that most dieters cannot maintain their weight loss for as little as a year. Aerobic exercise, combined with sensible modifications in one's eating habits which can be sustained for a lifetime, is a very effective way to lose weight and keep it off. Exercise contributes to weight loss by burning calories, bringing appetite in line with energy expenditure and by maintaining or enhancing the resting metabolic rate.

There are few differences between the nutritional needs of active and inactive people. One notable difference between the two groups is the need for extra calories by the active people with an emphasis on increasing their intake of complex carbohydrates. The increased caloric consumption results in an increase in the intake of vitamins, minerals, carbohydrates, fats and protein. Nutritional supplements are generally unnecessary. It also appears that salt and potassium supplementation for active people is unnecessary since both are found in a wide variety of foods. Replacing the water lost in sweat is extremely important and active people must insure that they are maintaining a state of hydration.

Techniques have been developed for the measurement of body fat. Skinfold measures have been presented because they are practical, economical and relatively easy to learn. The percentage of the body's weight which is made up of fat must be known if one is to intelligently counsel another about how much weight to lose. Height-weight charts do not yield such information and should not be used for this purpose.

Spot reduction is a fallacy promoted by people with vested interests who have little regard for the buyer's interests.

REFERENCE

1. Costill, D. F. and others. "The Role of Dietary Carbohydrate in Muscle Glycogen Resynthesis After Strenuous Running." *American Journal of Clinical Nutrition*, 34: 1831, 1981.

2. Hultman, E. "Studies on Muscle Metabolism of Glycogen and Active Phosphate in Man with Special Reference to Exercise and Diet," *Scandinavian Journal of Clinical Laboratory Investigation*, 19:94 (Supplement), 1967.

3. ADA Reports. "Position of the American Dietetic Association: Nutrition For Physical Fitness and Athletic Performance for Adults," *Journal of the American Dietetic Association*, Vol. 87: No. 7, 937, July, 1987.

4. U.S. Senate Select Committee On Nutrition and Human Needs. *Dietary Goals For the United States, 2nd Edition*, Washington, D. C.: Government Printing Office, 1977.

5. Whitney, E. N. and Hamilton, E. M. N. *Understanding Nutrition, 4th Edition*, St. Paul: West Publishing Co., 1987.

6. The American Institute For Cancer Research. "Dietary Guidelines to Lower Cancer Risk," AICR Information Series (pamphlet)

7. The American Institute for Cancer Research. "All About Fat and Cancer Risk," AICR Information Series, September, 1985.

8. Infections and Undernutrition. *Nutrition Reviews* 40:119, 1982.

9. Licata, A. A. "Acute Effects of Increased Meat Protein on Urinary Electrolytes and Cyclic Adinosine Monophosphate and Serum Parathyroid Hormone" *American Journal of Clinical Nutrition*, 34:1979, 1981.

10. Carroll, K. K. "Dietary Protein and Heart Disease" *Nutrition and the M.D.*, June, 1985.

11. The Select Committee on Nutrition and Human Needs. *Dietary Goals For the United States*, Washington, D.C.: U.S. Government Printing Office, 1977.

12. Fenner, L. "Salt Shakes Up Some of Us" *FDA Consumer*, March, 1980.

13. de Vries, H. A. *Health Science*, Santa Monica, California: Goodyear Publishing Co, 1979.

14. Stern, J. S. "Is Obesity a Disease of Inactivity?" *Food and Fitness*, 51, March, 1984.

15. Cooper, K. H. *The Aerobics Program For Total Well-Being*, New York: Bantam Books, 1982.

16. Barnes, H. V. "Study Shows 39 Percent Boys Overweight," *President's Council Newsletter*, Washington, D. C.: 3, August, 1977.

17. "Youth Fitness Status Report," *Forums on Youth Fitness*, American College of Sports Medicine, 5, 1982.

18. Mayer, J. "Obesity" in Goodhart, R. S. and Shils, M. E. *Modern Nutrition In Health and Disease*, Philadelphia: Lea and Febiger, 1980.

19. Wallis, C. "Gauging the Fat of the Land," *Time*, 72, February 25, 1985.

20. Wood, P. *California Diet and Exercise Program*, Mountain View, California: Anderson World Books, Inc., 1983

21. Wood, P. "The Science of Successful Weight Loss," *Food and Fitness*, 1:3, March, 1984.

22. Howley, E.T. and Franks, B. D. *Health/Fitness Instructor's Handbook*, Champaign, Il: Human Kinetics Publishers, Inc., 1986.

23. "Food and Obesity in the Rat" *Nutrition Reviews*, 37: 52, 1979.

24. "Obesity: the High Cost of Fat," *The Health Letter*, 2: No. 7, 1, 1973.

25. American Diabetes Association, *1984 Fact Sheet On Diabetes*, 1984.

26. Blouin, B. B. "Diet and Obesity," *Journal of the American Dietetic Association*, 70:535, 1977.

27. Harris, T. G. and Gurin, J. "Look Who's Getting It All Together," *American Health*, 42, March, 1985.

28. Gastineau, C. F. "Obesity: Risks, Causes and Treatment," *Medical Clinics of North America*, 56:1021, July, 1972.

29. "The Nutrition Gazette," *Nutrition Today*, 5, July/August, 1979.

30. Mayer, J. and others. "Relations Between Caloric Intake, Body Weight, and Physical Work: Studies In An Industrial Male Population In West Bengal," *American Journal of Clinical Nutritional*, 4:169, 1956.

31. Wood, P. D. and others. "Increased Exercise Level and Plasma Lipoprotein Concentrations: A One Year, Randomized, Controlled Study in Secondary Middle-Aged Men," *Metabolism*, 32:31, 1983.

32. Bullen, B. A. and others. "Physical Activity of Obese and Non-Obese Adolescent Girls Appraised By Motion Picture Sampling," *American Journal of Clinical Nutrition*, 4:211, 1964. to Energy Output of Obese and Non-Obese Adolescent Boys," *American Journal of Clinical Nutrition*, 7:55, 1964.

34. de Vries, H. A. "Physical Fitness Guidlines for Older Adults," *President's Council On Physical Fitness and Sports Newsletter*, Washington, D.C.: March, 1980.

35. Brozck, J. and Keys, A. "Relative Body Weight, Age, and Fitness," *Geratrics*, 8:70, February, 1953.

36. Schultz, C. and others. "Effects of Severe Caloric Restriction and Moderate Exercise on Basal Metabolic Rate and Hormonal Status in Adult Humans," *Federal Proceedings*, 39:783, 1980.

37. Zuti, B. and Golding L. "Comparing Diet and Exercise As Weight Reduction Tools," *The Physician And Sportsmedicine*, 4: No. 1, 49, 1976.

CHAPTER FOUR

Physiological Adaptations To Jogging

ACUTE ADAPTATIONS

Acute adaptations to jogging refer to those physiological changes which occur during and after a single bout of exercise. It is important to recognize these adjustments and understand that they are temporary. Some selected acute physiological changes will be cursorily discussed.

Heart Rate

The heart's response to jogging is immediate. The rate of beating increases with the first strides and continues to do so until a steady state has been achieved. Steady state (leveling off of heart rate) only occurs when the intensity of the workout is within the individual's capacity. It represents a period during jogging when the oxygen demand of the activity can be supplied by the body on a minute-by-minute basis.

Steady state cannot be achieved when the intensity of the workout is beyond the participant's ability to supply all of the oxygen required. In this instance, the jogger goes into oxygen debt (oxygen in excess of the resting value used in recovery to replace the deficit incurred during exercise). Such a pace can only be tolerated for short periods of time as it produces high heart rates and elevated levels of lactic acid (a fatiguing metabolite resulting from the incomplete breakdown of sugar).

Elevating the heart rate represents the major vehicle for increasing blood flow, and therefore oxygen, to the muscles during exercise. The heart rate for any workload will be higher for a given individual when he or she is in an untrained state.

Stroke Volume

Stroke volume refers to the amount of blood that the heart can eject in one beat. The size of the stroke volume is dependent upon the amount of blood returning to the heart, the dimensions of the systemic pumping chamber (left ventricle), and the force of the contraction. Stroke volume rises linearly; that is, it is positively correlated with increases in workload up to forty to sixty percent of capacity and then levels off.[1] From this point on, further increases in blood flow occur as the result of increases in heart rate. The higher stroke volume of trained people represents one of the major differences between them and the untrained and accounts for their ability to sustain endurance activities.

Cardiac Output

Cardiac output (Q) represents the amount of blood pumped by the heart in one minute. It is the product of heart rate and stroke volume ($Q = HR \times SV$). The cardiac output increases as the intensity of exercise increases. Initially, it increases because both heart rate and stroke volume increase. Stroke volume levels off when exercise reaches approximately fifty percent of capacity, so further increases in cardiac output are due to elevations in heart rate.

The average value for cardiac output at rest is approximately four to six liters of blood per minute with values reaching twenty to twenty-five liters during maximal exercise. Well-conditioned athletes can achieve as much as forty liters during very high-intensity work.

Blood Flow

The body has the remarkable capacity to shunt blood to tissues that have the greatest need. For example, blood flow to the working muscles increases during physical activity. This is accomplished because blood flow to other tissues and organs such as the liver, kidneys and digestive system is reduced. In the competition for available blood, the muscles take precedence during physical activity. Blood flow to the digestive system is increased after a meal because this represents the greatest area of need. But if physical activity occurs immediately after eating, blood will be shunted away from the digestive system to the muscles. Digestion will slow down or stop depending upon the severity of the exercise. This is one of the major reasons why a workout should not begin until at least one hour after a meal.

More blood than usual is shunted to the skin during hot weather to help cool the body. The skin competes with the exercising muscles for the available blood, which results in the muscles receiving slightly less than normal. Less blood means less oxygen and nutrients for exercise and the workout becomes more difficult. This is why exercise in hot weather should be less vigorous and last for a shorter period of time.

Blood Pressure

Systolic pressure, which is measured when the heart contracts and sends blood into the aorta, rises with exercise. It can increase from resting levels of 120 mmHg to 200 mmHg and beyond with very intense exercise. This is a normal response as long as the pressure does not get well above 200 mmHg. The marked rise in systolic blood pressure is due to the increase in cardiac output that is necessary to maintain blood flow to the heart and brain as well as supplying the needs of the working muscles and skin. The blood vessels in the working muscles dilate to accommodate more blood while the vessels in inactive tissues constrict. On the surface, this adjustment seems to indicate some reduction in blood pressure but the four-to-five-fold increase in cardiac output overcomes the blood vessels' ability to distend and increases systolic pressure.

Diastolic pressure during dynamic exercise changes very little (less than 10 mmHg) or not at all. An increase of 15 mmHg or more in diastolic pressure indicates a greater likelihood of coronary artery disease.[2] However, static or isometric exercises, where forceful contractions are held in a fixed position for several seconds, increases diastolic as well as systolic pressures. The rise is due to the increased resistance of statically contracting muscles.

Blood Volume

Fluid is removed from all areas of the body in order to produce the perspiration needed to cool the exerciser. Some of this fluid comes from the blood plasma, which reduces blood volume. The hematocrit, which is the volume percent of red blood cells, increases due to the reduction in blood volume. This increases the viscosity of the blood and inhibits the delivery of oxygen. The hematocrit returns to normal as fluids are consumed following the workout.

Respiratory Responses

The average person breathes twelve to sixteen times per minute at rest and forty to fifty times per minute during maximal exertion. Ventilation (V), the amount of air inhaled and exhaled per minute, is a product of the frequency of breathing (f) and the volume of air per breath or tidal volume (TV). At rest, the lungs typically ventilate five to six liters of air each minute. For example, fourteen breaths per minute at 0.4 liter per breath results in a ventilatory rate of 5.6 liters of air/minute.

$$V = f \times TV$$
$$= 14 \times 0.4 \text{ liters}$$
$$= 5.6 \text{ liters}$$

Ventilation may escalate to 100 liters or more during maximal exertion. Large, well-conditioned athletes may move as much as 200 liters per minute.

The movement of large volumes of air from the lungs during exercise places a burden upon the respiratory muscles. The energy cost of breathing during rest represents two percent of the total oxygen consumed, but during vigorous exercise the cost may rise to ten percent.[3]

Two respiratory phenomena, side-stitch and second wind, remain mysteries in terms of their etiology. A side-stitch is a pain in the side that may be severe enough to stop activity. Constant pressure applied with both hands at the site of the stitch may alleviate the pain and allow continued activity. Breathing deeply while extending the arms overhead may also provide some relief. Currently, there are two possible causes of side-stitch, spasm of the diaphragm due to diminished blood flow, and trapped gas, decrease in blood flow, or a combination of both in the large intestine.

Second wind is an adaptation in which the perceived effort of exercise appears to become considerably lessened although there is no change in the intensity level. The mechanisms involved are not completely understood but when second wind is achieved, breathing becomes less labored and participants experience a sense of comfort and well-being. Wilmore states that "it is possibly a result of more efficient circulation to the active tissues or of a more efficient metabolic process."[1]

Metabolic Responses

Metabolism increases with the inception of exercise and continues to do so in direct proportion to increases in exercise intensity. Metabolism may be measured indirectly with appropriate equipment by the amount of oxygen consumed during exercise on a treadmill, bicycle ergometer, or other similar devices. When the intensity of exercise steadily increases the individual's ability to supply the oxygen needed to keep pace will eventually plateau. This plateau represents the upper limit of endurance and is referred to as maximal oxygen consumption (Max VO_2). Also known as aerobic capacity or circulorespiratory endurance, it defines a point where further increases in exercise intensity do not elicit further increases in oxygen consumption. (see Figure 4.1)

FIGURE 4.1 Oxygen Uptake By Trained and Untrained People

This figure illustrates the difference in response to exercise between the trained and the untrained.

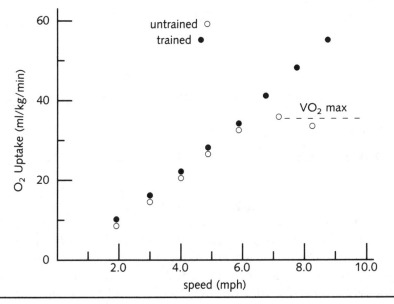

Max VO_2 represents the body's peak ability to assimilate, deliver and extract oxygen and it is considered to be the best indicator of physical fitness. It is a well-defined exercise endpoint that can be measured and reproduced accurately in the laboratory. These procedures are not generally available to the public, but fortunately field tests have been developed that correlate fairly well with the lab tests and may substitute for them. These will be discussed later in this chapter.

Max VO_2 is measured in liters of oxygen utilized per minute. This absolute value is influenced considerably by body size. Since oxygen is needed and used by all body tissues, larger people take in and use more oxygen both at rest and during exercise. Aerobic capacity, when expressed in liters of oxygen per minute, is not conducive to comparison as it will yield spurious results. To eliminate the influence of size, aerobic capacity must be considered in terms of oxygen utilization per unit of body mass. This is accomplished by converting liters of oxygen to milliliters and then dividing by body weight in kilograms. For example, a 220 pound subject uses 4.5 liters of O_2 per minute during maximum exertion, while a 143 pound subject's capacity is 3.5 liters of O_2 per minute. From these data it appears that the larger subject is more aerobically fit due to a greater capacity to use oxygen, but observe what occurs when these values are corrected for body size. Divide body weight in pounds by 2.2 to convert to kilograms:

$$\frac{220 \text{ lbs.}}{2.205 \text{ kg.}} \quad = \quad 100 \text{ kg.}$$

Subject 1. 4.5 LO_2/min. = 4500 ml. O_2/min.

4500 ml. O_2/min. ÷ 100 kg. (200 lbs.) = 45ml. O_2/kg/min.

Subject 2. 3.5 LO_2/min. = 3500 ml. O_2/min.

3500 ml. O_2/min. ÷ 65 kg. (143 lbs.) = 54ml. O_2/kg/min.

It's obvious from this example that the lighter subject can transport, extract, and use more oxygen per unit of body mass than the larger subject and is better equipped to perform endurance activities. Max VO_2 values expressed in ml O_2/kg/min. range from the mid-20s in sedentary older people to 94, which is the highest documented value recorded thus far. This enormous capacity belongs to an extremely well-conditioned male cross-country skier. The highest value recorded for female athletes is 74, also by a cross-country skier. College-age females have values in the upper thirties to low forties.

Max VO_2 is affected by age, sex, body composition, heredity, and type of training. Sex differences in aerobic capacity become evident after puberty with females exhibiting lower max VO_2 values. The difference is attributed to smaller heart size per unit of body weight, less oxygen-carrying capacity due to lower blood hemoglobin concentration, less muscle tissue, and more body fat. However, there is considerable overlap between the sexes regarding aerobic capacity. World-class females competing in endurance events are aerobically superior to most males but they have lower values than world class male competitors. The differences between males and females are probably a combination of true physiological limitations and cultural restraints that have been placed upon females regarding endurance training and competition. The influence of culture and biology on female performance will eventually become clearer as more females train and compete during the next decade.

Aerobic capacity increases with age to the late teens or early twenties and then begins to decline quite systematically by approximately ten percent per decade for sedentary people and somewhat less for active people. See Figure 4.2.

The decline in aerobic capacity with age may be partially attributable to the problems associated with the assessment of maximum performance in older people. Prudent exercise scientists who are reluctant to push elderly subjects to exhaustion as well as the fear of overexertion, lack of motivation, and muscular weakness experienced by many older people may operate together to cause underestimation of maximum capacity. But regardless of measurement problems, the decline in Max VO_2 seems to parallel the functional losses that occur as a result of the aging process. Maximum heart rate, cardiac output, and metabolism decrease during the adult years. Body composition changes as muscle tissue is lost, thus decreasing the body's energy-producing machinery.

Fat tissue is gained, which is an impediment to physical performance. Ventilatory capacity deceases as the thoracic cage (chest) loses some of its elasticity due to weakened intercostal muscles (muscles between the ribs), increased residual volume (air remaining in the lungs after expiration), and increased rigidity of lung structures. Many of these changes can be delayed or at

FIGURE 4.2   Decline in Max VO$_2$ With Age

This figure illustrates the decline in Max VO$_2$ with age for active and inactive people.

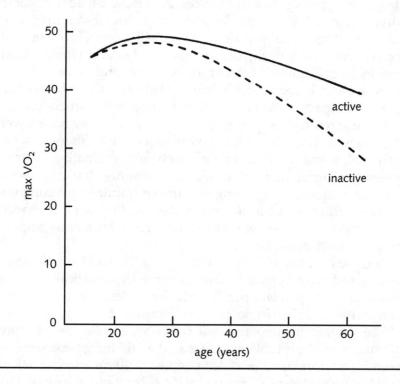

least slowed down by a physically active lifestyle, as is exemplified by Figure 4.2. Active sixty-year-olds exhibit max VO$_2$ levels comparable to inactive thirty-year-olds. The effects of training and heredity will be treated in greater detail later in this chapter.

When exercise begins, a short interval of time is needed for the body to adjust to the increased oxygen demand. This period, when the oxygen demand of exercise exceeds the body's transport capability, is referred to as the oxygen deficit (see Figure 4.3).

A second phenomenon, oxygen debt, occurs during both aerobic and anaerobic exercise (see Figure 4.3). Oxygen debt refers to the amount of oxygen consumed during the exercise recovery period which is above that normally consumed at rest. It is measured at the end of exercise and includes the O$_2$ deficit. During anaerobic exercise the body cannot supply all of the O$_2$ needed, resulting in a deficiency between supply and demand that must

FIGURE 4.3 O_2 Deficit and O_2 Debt (Energy Debt)

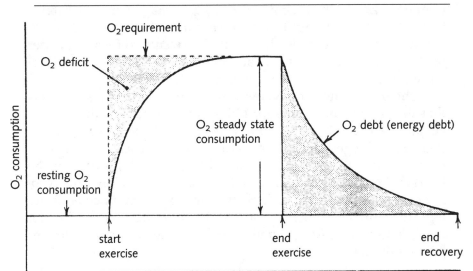

be repaid at the end of exercise. A ten-second sprint or a run up two or three flights of stairs elevates heart rate and ventilation. Both persist for a few moments following the activity before gradually returning to resting levels. The extra oxygen consumed during this interval represents the O_2 debt. Aerobic exercise also produces an O_2 debt that may be entirely due to the O_2 deficit, particularly in low-intensity exercise. Aerobic exercise that is in excess of fifty percent of the aerobic capacity will produce lactic acid and a further increase in O_2 debt.

CHRONIC ADAPTATIONS

The chronic adaptations, also referred to as the long-term effects, are those physiological and psychological changes that are the result of training. These changes represent the training effect that is gradually developed after repeated bouts of exercise.

Heart Rate

A few months of jogging will produce a decrease in the resting heart rate (RHR) by ten to twenty-five beats per minute. The decrease in resting heart rate is accompanied by a decline in exercise heart rate for a given workload. For example, a jogging speed which elicits a heart rate of 150 beats per minute prior to training may invoke a heart rate of 125 beats per minute after a few months of training. Five to six months of training will lower the submaximum exercise heart rate by twenty to forty beats per minute. Also, the exercise heart rate returns to the resting level more rapidly as physical fitness improves.

The importance of lowered resting and exercise heart rates is that this allows more time for filling the ventricles with blood to be pumped to all of the body's tissues and more time for the delivery of oxygen and nutrients to the heart muscle. The delivery of these substances occurs during diastole (resting phase of the heart cycle) because relaxation of the heart muscle allows the coronary vessels to open up and receive the blood that it needs. Training substantially prolongs the heart's diastolic phase. The net result is that the heart operates more efficiently and with longer periods of rest.

Stroke Volume

Stroke volume and heart rate are inversely related; as stroke volume increases heart rate decreases. The heart rate at rest and for a given workload is less because of the heart's enhanced ability to pump more blood per beat. This is accomplished because of more complete filling of the left ventricle combined with an increase in the contractile strength of its muscular walls, resulting in a more forceful contraction and greater emptying of the blood in the chamber. This stronger, more efficient heart is capable of meeting circulatory challenges with less beats both at rest and during submaximum exercise.

Cardiac Output

Post-training cardiac output is increased considerably during maximum exercise, but there is little change during rest or submaximum work primarily because the trained individual is able to extract more oxygen from the blood. The oxygen concentration in arterial blood is essentially unchanged but the extraction rate (a-VO_2 difference) may be increased significantly. With training the a-VO_2 difference is increased, resulting in more oxygen being used as reflected by less oxygen in the venous blood.

Blood Flow

Training produces an increase in blood volume and a concomitant increase in the total number of red blood cells. However, the red blood cells do not increase proportionately to blood volume so on a per unit of blood basis, the red cells appear to have decreased in number. In fact, many distance runners and long time joggers may, upon medical examination, appear to be anemic. They actually possess an above-normal total number of red blood cells but relative values per 100ml of blood which are below normal. This adaptation to the stress of jogging is an important one because the lowered viscosity (stickiness) of the blood in the trained state facilitates the delivery of oxygen to working muscles.

Blood Pressure

Jogging and other aerobic exercise contribute to blood pressure control. Studies which have only examined the effects of occupational energy expenditure on blood pressure control have produced conflicting results. But Montoye and his group considered both leisure and occupational energy expenditure and found that the least active men had the highest systolic and diastolic blood pressures.[4] Ten years of data collection at the Georgia Baptist Medical Center's exercise program indicated that both systolic and diastolic pressures were reduced for program participants.[5]

It is quite clear that the lower the blood pressure within the normal range, the lower the risk. Blood pressures below 90/60 are considered to be abnormally low. Traditionally, the upper limits of normal are 130/90 for men under the age of 45, 140/95 for men over 45, and 160/95 for women over 45. But people whose pressure borders on these values have a fifty percent increase in death rate compared to those whose values are at more desirable levels.[7] Optimal blood pressure should be lower than 120/74. People whose systolic pressure is between 131 and 138 have a 1.7 times greater risk for heart disease than if their pressure is 120. A systolic pressure of 105 decreases the risk still further. When the diastolic pressure is between 85 and 94, those affected are 1.8 times as likely to have heart disease than if this pressure is 75. With blood pressure, lower is definitely better.

The physiological mechanisms involved in lowering blood pressure through exercise are not fully understood, but there are several possible explanations. First, arteriosclerosis (hardening of the arteries) is a disease in which the arterial muscles and connective lining lose their elasticity. The arteries become progressively more inflexible and more pressure is required to move blood through them. Endurance exercise may counteract this process because arterial muscles must contract and relax in order to shunt blood to those areas of greatest need while we exercise. As a result, we exercise the arterial muscles at the same time that we are exercising the skeletal muscles. Endurance exercise has a vasodilating (opening up) effect on the blood vessels and this may help them to retain their elasticity. Secondly, atherosclerosis (a buildup of plaque along, arterial walls) narrows the channel, increases resistance to blood flow, and increases blood pressure. Fats, particularly cholesterol, are involved in the development of plaque. Endurance exercises may retard this process because more of the circulating fat is used for fuel, which means that there is less available for deposit along the arterial walls. Third, the trained heart may be less sensitive to adrenalin, so blood pressure does not rise precipitously in response.

Heart Volume

The heart reacts to persistent jogging in much the same manner as the other muscles of the body react to regular exercise. It becomes stronger, and oftentimes, larger. The volume as well as the weight of the heart increases with endurance training. Bed rest produces the opposite effect. Prior to bed rest the average heart volume of five young male subjects was 867 milliliters (ml).[7] Twenty days of bed rest reduced the volume to 778 ml. Bed rest was followed by fifty days of training that increased the volume to 900 ml. Many other studies have confirmed the change in heart volume as a result of jogging.

Respiratory Responses

Some training-induced adaptations also occur in the respiratory system. The muscles that support breathing improve in both strength and endurance. This increases the amount of air that can be expired after a maximum inspiration (vital capacity) and decreases the amount of air remaining in the lungs (residual volume). Ventilation decreases slightly for a given workload and increases significantly during maximum exercise as a result of training. This indicates an improvement in the efficiency of the system.

The depth of each breath (tidal volume) also increases during vigorous exercise.

Training increases blood flow in the lungs. In the sitting or standing position, many of the pulmonary capillaries in the upper regions of the lungs close down because gravity pulls blood down to the lower portions of the lungs. Exercise forces blood into the upper lobes and creates a greater surface area for the diffusion of oxygen from the alveoli (air sacs) to the pulmonary blood. Perfusion of the upper lobes of the lungs is improved with training.

Metabolic Responses

Training may improve aerobic capacity by fifteen to twenty percent in a previously untrained healthy young adult. The improvement is due to a combination of physiological adaptations resulting from several months of aerobic training. First, the number and size of mitochondria increase. The mitochondria (often referred to as the cells' powerhouse) are organelles within the cells that utilize oxygen to produce the ATP needed by the muscles. Second, enzymes that are located within the mitochondria and that accelerate the chemical reactions needed for the production of ATP are increased. These increases in the mitochondria and their enzymes produce greater amounts of energy and an improvement in physical fitness. Third, there is an increase in maximal cardiac output and local blood perfusion in the exercising muscles. Training increases the arterial-venous oxygen difference a-VO$_2$ diff), which reflects the ability of the muscles to extract oxygen from the blood. At rest the oxygen content of arterial blood is approximately 20 ml per 100 ml of blood, while the oxygen content of venous blood is approximately 14 ml per 100 ml of blood. The O$_2$ difference between the two is 6 ml (20ml O$_2$ – 14 ml O$_2$ = 6 ml O$_2$) representing the amount of O$_2$ that was extracted (the a-VO$_2$ diff) by the body during rest. Exercise of increasing intensity results in a progressive widening of the difference as the body uses more of the delivered oxygen. The amount of O$_2$ in the venous blood decreases while the amount in arterial blood remains relatively unchanged. During strenuous exercise the oxygen content of venous blood approaches zero in the exercising muscles but it rarely drops below 2 ml when mixed venous blood is sampled in the right atrium of the heart. The reason for this phenomenon is that blood from the exercising muscles mixes with blood coming from inactive tissues as it returns to the heart. The a-VO$_2$ diff during maximum exercise but may not increase it at rest and during submaximum exercise.

Aerobic capacity is finite. Each of us is endowed with an aerobic potential limited by our heredity. A small percentage of people inherit the potential to achieve amazing feats of endurance as exemplified by performances in marathons, ultramarathons, Iron Man Triathalons, cross-country runs lasting weeks or months, and long-distance bike races. Most of us are in the average category for aerobic capacity but all of us can achieve our potential with endurance training. At this point aerobic capacity will level off and remain unchanged even if training is intensified. However, aerobic performance will improve with harder training. The following example which applies to both sexes illustrates this point. Let's assume that a female jogger has achieved her aerobic potential of 60ml/kg/min with two years of hard training. At this point she is able to jog a five-mile course at a 42ml/kg/min pace, or seventy percent of her aerobic capacity. After three more years of vigorous training (Max VO$_2$ still at 60ml/kg/min) she is now able to sustain a 53ml/kg/min pace, or eighty-eight percent of her aerobic capacity. The extra three years of training has permitted her to use more oxygen, thereby sustaining a faster pace for the course without dipping materially into anaerobic fuels that produce lactic acid and oxygen debt. The point during exercise where blood lactate begins to increase is defined as the anaerobic threshold. Training moves the anaerobic threshold closer to the max VO$_2$ and allows the participant to exercise at a higher percentage of capacity. Two people with the same max VO$_2$ will perform differently if one has an anaerobic threshold substantially higher than the other.

UNPROVEN TRAINING EFFECTS

Coronary Collateral Circulation

Coronary collateral circulation refers to the development of tiny blood vessels in the heart muscle. This network of new vessels can supply those portions of the heart muscle whose normal complement of blood has to some extent been reduced by disease. The development of coronary capillaries can enhance the delivery of oxygen because more blood is coursing through the myocardium and the capillaries are closer to the muscle fibers, thus facilitating the diffusion of oxygen to the muscle cells. Theoretically, these new vessels would protect against a heart attack and enhance survival and recovery should a heart attack occur.

Several animal studies have shown that coronary collateral circulation occurs in response to exercise, while other studies have been unable to show this development. The precise stimulus that may initiate the development of collateral circulation is still unknown. Evidence indicates that it might be due to the physical stimulus of vigorous exercise, or due to hypoxia (deficiency of oxygen) during exercise, or diminished blood supply from the atherosclerotic process, or it may be the result of some chemical trigger.

There is no evidence at the present time to support the notion of coronary collateral development in "normal" human subjects. People who have suffered heart attacks have been studied with coronary arteriographic techniques. The results indicated that there was no difference in collateral growth between exercising and nonexercising subjects.[8, 9] But one of these investigators correctly stated that coronary arteriography may not be sensitive enough to detect the growth of collateral vessels. At any rate, it appears that coronary collaterals do not develop in human hearts as a result of training. Better assessment techniques and more sensitive instruments are needed before a definitive statement can be made regarding collateral circulation. While we wait for this to occur, the best advice would be to begin exercising now. Don't wait for proof positive because it may be a long time in coming. The implications of collateral circulation development for heart health are enormous. Even if future research unequivocally shows that collateral circulation does not occur in humans, the other benefits of physical activity are reason enough to establish the exercise habit.

Coronary Vessel Size

Endurance training seems to enlarge the diameter of the coronary blood vessels of animals as indicated by several studies. This phenomenon is much more difficult to study in humans, but the implications of this adaptation for heart attack prevention is significant. Probably the case most often discussed regarding coronary vessel size is that of Clarence DeMar. He was a distance runner virtually all of his adult life and competed in more than

1000 distance races in his career. He ran the Boston Marathon 34 times and won 7 of these. He died of cancer at the age of 70. An autopsy revealed that while his coronary arteries exhibited some atherosclerosis their diameters were so large — two to three times normal size — that blood flow through them would not have been impeded for decades. Many have speculated that his enlarged arteries were due to a lifetime of running, but there is no way to establish that fact. The reason for his large vessels could conceivably be that he was born with that endowment although there was nothing in his family history to account for such an unusual physical development. Hutchins and his coworkers found that there was a positive relationship between the weight of the heart and the diameters of the coronary vessels that service it. That being the case, it may be more than a reasonable possibility that DeMar's large arteries were related to his larger, heavier heart (which was probably the product of a lifetime of exercise).

Cause-and-effect relationships between exercise and coronary vessel size remain elusive in humans. Extrapolating from animal studies to humans is risky, but the fact that this phenomenon has occurred in animals raises hope for the same response in human beings.

THE PHYSIOLOGICAL EFFECTS OF DETRAINING

The effects of detraining were documented in a recent study using subjects who had trained hard and continuously for ten years and then disrupted their training for 84 days.[10] Most of their aerobic capacity was lost after 21 days of inactivity and continued to decrease for the next 35 days where it stabilized at 16 percent below the trained level. Stroke volume decreased 10 to 14 percent during the first 21 days and continued to decline until it reached a level compatible with a group of sedentary "controls" by the end of the study.

Oxidative enzymes in the muscles decreased 40 percent at the end of eight weeks. At the end of the 84-day period, the researchers had the subjects perform a sub-maximum bout of exercise. The changes which resulted from detraining were reflected in their response to this bout of exercise. There was an 18 percent increase in oxygen consumption in the detrained state compared to the trained state, a 17 percent increase in heart rate (185 beats/min detrained compared to 158 beat/min trained), 24 percent increase in ventilation, a six percent increase in the respiratory quotient which indicated a greater reliance upon carbohydrate metabolism, and a 34 percent increase of perceived exertion (Borg scale). This effort produced six times as much lactic acid in the detrained state compared to the trained state. Most of the benefits achieved during 10 years of training were lost or substantially eroded with 84 days of detraining.

SUMMARY

This chapter has focused upon the acute and chronic changes which occur in the human body as the result of exercise. The acute effects of jogging involve those changes which occur during and after a single bout of exercise. These bodily adjustments to jogging are temporary. The chronic adaptations, which are the long-term effects of jogging, represent the training effect that is gradually developed after repeated bouts of exercise. Emphasized were those changes which occur to the heart, circulation, respiration and metabolism. The effects of detraining were also examined.

REFERENCES

1. Wilmore, J. H. *Training for Sport and Activity*, Boston: Allyn and Bacon, Inc., 1982.
2. Sheps, D. "Exercise-Induced Increase In Diastolic Pressure: Indication of Severe Coronary Artery Disease," *American Journal of Cardiology*, 43:708, 1979.
3. Astrand, P. O. and Rodahl. *Textbook of Work Physiology*, New York: McGraw-Hill Book Co., 1977.
4. Montoye, H. J. and others. "Habitual Physical Activity and Blood Pressure," *Medicine and Science in Sports*, Winter: 175, 1972.
5. Fletcher, G. F. *Exercise in the Practice of Medicine*, New York: Futura Publishing Co., 1982.
6. Lamb, L. (ed.). "Your Vital Blood Pressure," *The Health Letter*, 15: No. 8, April 25, 1980.
7. Saltin, B. and others. "Response To Submaximal and Maximal Exercise After Bed Rest and Training," *Circulation*, 38:Supplement 7, 1968.
8. Barnard, R. J. "Long-Term Effects of Exercise On Cardiac Function," *Exercise and Sport Science Review*, 3:113, 1975.
9. Ferguson, R. J. and others. "Coronary Arteriography and Treadmill Exercise Capacity Before and After 13 Months of Physical Training," *Medicine and Science in Sports*, 5:67, 1973.
10. Coyle, E. F. and others. "Time Course of Loss of Adaptations After Stopping Prolonged Intense Endurance Training," *Journal of Applied Physiology*, 57:1857, 1984.

CHAPTER FIVE

Health Benefits of Jogging

INTRODUCTION

According to Falls, "Health-related fitness refers to those aspects of physiological and psychological functioning which are believed to offer some protection against degenerative type diseases such as coronary heart disease, obesity, and various musculoskeletal disorders."[1] The effect of long-term participation in jogging upon these types of diseases will be discussed in this chapter.

Health-related fitness, consisting of cardiorespiratory endurance, muscular strength, muscular endurance, and flexibility, has a profound effect upon body composition. Decreasing the amount of stored fat while concomitantly increasing muscle mass is highly desirable and mounting evidence seems to indicate that it definitely has an impact upon the quality of life and may positively affect the quantity of life.

JOGGING'S EFFECT UPON THE CORONARY RISK FACTORS

The American Heart Association has identified cigarette smoking, hypertension (high blood pressure) and hypercholesteremia (elevated blood cholesterol) as the primary coronary risk factors. Fortunately, these risks can be modified by practicing healthy living habits, such as consistent and appropriate exercise, weight loss, low fat-high complex carbohydrate diet, salt restriction, medical screening, and commitment and willpower.

Secondary risk factors which may also be modified include obesity, inactivity, stress and diabetes. The strategies discussed in the previous paragraph also apply to these risk factors.

Risk factors which cannot be changed include heredity, race, sex and age. First-degree relatives who die prematurely from heart disease would indicate a significant family history and a substantial risk. First-degree relatives are parents, grandparents, and siblings who die prior to the age of 60 of heart disease.

Females are less prone than males to heart disease; this is particularly true during the child-bearing years. There are several reasons for this phenomenon: (1) the female hormone estrogen tends to protect the arteries from premature destruction, and (2) females have a higher average HDL-C (high density lipoproteins) than males. HDL-C prevents the formation of atherosclerosis which is discussed later in this chapter.

Age is positively correlated with death from heart disease. Seventy-five percent of all cardiovascular deaths occur after the age of 65.[1] The study of aging is complicated for many reasons, one of which is that it is difficult to separate the changes which are true indices of aging from those that are associated with disuse atrophy. The body thrives upon proper amounts and types of exercise. Since active people are more energetic, slimmer and younger in appearance than inactive people, we might conclude that they are aging according to the way that nature intended. A sedentary lifestyle tends to accentuate those changes that are reflective of aging.

Racial influences upon heart disease are not quite as clearly defined. Black Americans appear to be more susceptible to heart disease and stroke, probably due to the pervasive hypertension found among them,[2] but the Blacks of South Africa and Haiti have a very low incidence of heart disease.[3] Native Japanese have the lowest saturated fat consumption in the industrialized world as well as the lowest mortality from cardiovascular disease.[4] Japanese who migrate to the United States and adopt American dietary habits increase their likelihood of developing cardiovascular disease.[5] It is difficult to separate cultural influences from racial influences regarding the incidence of mortality from cardiovascular disease.

Although heredity, sex, age, and race affect the incidence of cardiovascular disease, their influence may be mitigated by living a healthy lifestyle. In fact, it is imperative for people who are affected with unchangeable risk factors to avoid living habits which contribute to their predisposition for heart disease.

Cholesterol

Chemically, cholesterol is classified as a sterol (a solid alcohol). Although it is closely related, it is not a true fat and contains no calories. A certain amount of cholesterol is necessary for good health — it is important for proper digestion, hormone production, cell membrane activity and it is one of the structural components of nerve tissue. However, too much cholesterol in the blood stream creates a risk for heart disease and stroke. How much is too much? The National Heart, Lung, and Blood Institute now believes that people under 30 years of age should reduce their blood cholesterol below 180mg/dl (180 milligrams per deciliter of blood) and that those who are older should reduce their levels below 200mg/dl. The incidence of coronary artery disease increases substantially when cholesterol levels are above 220mg/dl.[6] Results from the 35-year-old Framingham Heart Study indicated that none of the 5000 subjects with a blood cholesterol level below 150mg/dl ever had a heart attack.[7]

It is important to keep total cholesterol within the guidelines outlined above but this represents only a part of the risk picture. Cholesterol is transporated in the blood stream by protein carriers called lipoproteins. Low density lipoproteins (LDL) consist of 25 percent protein, 45 percent cholesterol, with the remainder made up of other fats. Low density lipoproteins deposit some of their cholesterol in the artery walls creating a disease condition (atherosclerosis) which leads to heart attack and strokes.

Atherosclerosis is a slow progressive disease of the arteries which often has its origins in childhood. The process begins when the arterial lining becomes roughened and acts as an anchoring point for the deposit of cholesterol and other particles in the blood stream. These deposits, referred to as plaque, continue to grow over many years thereby narrowing the channel through which blood must flow. Eventually the channel will be blocked and a heart attack or stroke will occur. The higher the LDL blood level, the higher the risk.

High density lipoproteins (HDL) are made up of 45 to 50 percent protein and only 20 percent cholesterol with the remainder consisting of other fats. High density lipoproteins act as scavengers by attaching to cholesterol in the blood stream and peripheral cells. They transport cholesterol back to the liver where it is degraded and either excreted from the body in the feces or recycled to perform normal bodily functions. It is quite obvious that the risk of heart attack and stroke is reduced by decreasing total cholesterol and LDL and by increasing HDL.

A low level of HDL is an independent risk for cardiovascular disease. For males the risk increases when HDL is 30mg/dl or lower. The average value for males is 45mg/dl. For females the risk increases when HDL is 35mg/dl or below. The average values for females is 55mg/dl.

Another way to assess the cholesterol risk is to examine the ratio between total cholesterol (TC) and HDL. The average risk for males is a ratio of 5.0, while the average risk for females is 4.5. The number is attained by dividing total cholesterol by HDL. The lower the ratio, the lower the risk. When you have your cholesterol level checked, be sure that the analysis includes LDL, HDL, TC and the ratio between TC and HDL.

How does exercise, and jogging in particular, fit into the picture? Jogging is a significant contributor to weight loss, and weight loss is almost always accompanied by a decrease in TC and LDL. Sensible modifications in eating habits will also contribute to reducing weight and TC and LDL.

Jogging increases HDLs. Investigators working in the Stanford Heart Disease Prevention Program found that middle-aged male distance runners had higher HDL levels than their sedentary age-related peers.[8] The average distance jogged in this study was a modest 15 miles per week. This study established the threshold level required for HDL to increase. These data showed that the minimum weekly mileage needed to increase HDL was 10 miles and it took nine months to begin to see a change. Some of the subjects jogged 20 to 25 miles per week. Their HDL increases were larger than those who jogged less mileage which suggests that the more we jog (up to a point) the higher our HDL level. Other studies have shown a consistent relationship between jogging, as well as other forms of aerobic exercise, and an increase in HDL cholesterol.

Triglycerides

Triglycerides are found in food, may be synthesized by the liver and intestines, and constitute the most "space-efficient" form of energy storage in the body. Most of the fat in the body is stored in the form of triglycerides. These are composed of fatty acids of varying lengths that are attached to a molecule of glycerol.

Triglycerides, like cholesterol, are transported in the blood by protein carriers. Very-low-density lipoproteins (VLDL), made by the liver and intestine, transport fats, mostly triglycerides, in the blood.[9] Normal triglyceride levels range between 10 and 150 mg/100 ml of blood. Values above 150mg/100 ml are considered to be a risk factor for heart disease, but at this time it is considered to be a minor risk.

Exercise is an effective way to reduce triglyceride levels. One bout of exercise can reduce blood levels for 48 to 72 hours.[10] Jogging four to five times per week is very effective in suppressing blood triglycerides.

Blood Pressure

According to the American Heart Association, "high blood pressure is a silent, mysterious killer . . . silent because it has no characteristic symptoms; mysterious because, in more than 90 percent of the cases, the cause is unknown, and there is no cure. If hypertension is not controlled, serious cardiovascular complications may result."[1]

Hypertension can usually be controlled with medication, salt restriction, weight loss, and exercise. Since medications for controlling blood pressure may produce undesirable side effects, a better strategy might concentrate upon salt restriction, weight control, and exercise supplemented with such stress reduction techniques as progressive muscle relaxation, Benson's relaxation response, Transcendental Meditation, Yoga, and biofeedback. There is no guarantee that blood pressure can be normalized without medication, but many people have experienced success utilizing these approaches. Control without drugs is highly desirable.

A number of investigators have found that physical exercise of an aerobic nature can lower the pressures of hypertensive and borderline hypertensive men. To go a step further, can exercise reduce the blood pressure of "normotensives" or people with normal blood pressure? Would there be an advantage to lowering the pressure when it already is within normal range? With regard to the first question, the answer is uncertain. However, several studies have found that the diastolic pressure of normotensives was reduced at the end of an exercise program,[11] that both systolic and diastolic pressures were reduced in older (average age 69.5) normotensive men with exercise,[12] and that both systolic and diastolic pressures were reduced in a 10-year observance of the Georgia Baptist Medical Center's exercise program.[13]

McGarthy summarized the literature relating exercise and blood pressure this way: "It appears that older subjects (over 30) and persons with low initial fitness levels manifest decreases, whereas younger more fit subjects show little or no change. In addition, several studies on borderline and severe hypertensives have shown that reductions in blood pressure can occur with aerobic training.

Question number two is much easier to answer. It is quite clear that the lower the blood pressure within the normal range, the lower the risk.

Cigarette Smoking

On November 17, 1983, the Surgeon General of the U.S., Everett Koop, M.D., released a report that focused upon the relationship between cigarette smoking and cardiovascular disease. Two of the salient points were: Cigarette smoking should be considered the most important of the known modifiable risk factors for coronary heart disease in the U.S., and up to 30 percent of all coronary heart disease deaths are related to smoking. "While lung cancer is the disease most linked to smoking in the mind of the public, the total number of cigarette-related deaths due to heart disease is much larger than the number of cigarette-related deaths due to lung cancer."[15]

Many medical authorities consider cigarette smoking to be the most potent risk factor for heart disease. Nicotine, a powerful stimulant, adversely affects the circulatory system in a number of ways. First, it raises the resting heart rate by 10 to 20 beats per minute, increasing the work of the heart. The 12,000 or so extra daily beats reduce the heart's resting time and consequently, the delivery time in which it receives oxygen and nutrients. Second, nicotine stimulates the flow of adrenalin, the "fight-or-flight" hormone, which readies us for physical action. In the absence of a physical response, adrenalin circulates in the blood stream and eventually stores itself in the heart muscle where its action is analogous to carbon dust on an auto engine. Adrenalin stored in this manner causes the heart to become less efficient, increases the resting heart rate, and increases the amount of oxygen needed for a given workload. Third, nicotine produces a vasospastic (constricting) effect upon the blood vessels located in the extremities. Finger temperature may decline by 5 degrees or more after a cigarette due to peripheral blood vessel constriction. Usually, blood pressure also rises after a cigarette.

Cigarette smoking also may cause the heart to enlarge and skip beats. It increases blood platelet stickiness, shortening coagulation time and heightening the probability of blood clotting in the arteries. Blood platelets congregate at points of disease in the arteries where they release chemical substances which may precipitate a spasm. Such coronary spasms have been responsible for heart attacks in the absence of complete blood vessel occlusion.

Carbon monoxide, a second noxious product present in cigarette smoke, has a profound effect upon the heart and circulatory system. Hemoglobin, the iron-containing protein of the red blood cells that binds oxygen for transport in the blood stream, has a greater affinity for carbon monoxide than oxygen. Carbon monoxide, inhaled with every puff of a cigarette, occupies 5 to 10 percent of the smoker's hemoglobin. This lessens the blood's ability to carry oxygen to the tissues and explains in part the shortness of breath experienced by smokers during moderate exertion.

Lung cancer accounted for approximately 117,000 deaths in 1983. This represents about 25 percent of all cancer deaths and about 5 percent of all deaths in the U.S. More than 80 percent of these deaths are attributable to cigarette smoking.[16] These statistics were recently released by the American Cancer Society, which conclude that "cigarette smoking is the leading cause of cancer mortality in this country." Lung cancer remains among the least treatable forms of cancer.

The relationship between physical fitness and cigarette smoking behavior has been investigated. There is anecdotal evidence to suggest that smoking cessation follows the development of physical fitness. In a recent article, noted exercise scientist Jack Wilmore stated that, "Experts have also observed the major risk factors associated with heart disease — hypertension, high blood fat levels, even smoking — change in a positive direction as a result of an aerobic training program. (Few people who seriously engage in aerobic exercise continue to smoke.)"[17]

A random sample of 25,000 runners, most of them classified as recreational as opposed to competitive runners, who participated in the 1982 Atlanta Peachtree 10K (6.2 miles) race were surveyed regarding their perceptions of the effects of running upon their health.[18] Two major health benefits emerged: 1) weight loss was achieved, and 2) 81 percent of the male and 75 percent of the female smokers successfully quit the habit subsequent to the inception of their jogging program. There are thousands of testimonials indicating that people have successfully quit smoking when they began to participate regularly in an endurance exercise program, often after unsuccessfully trying a variety of other strategies. We have witnessed similar results in our Fitness and Wellness Center.

This type of evidence is abundant but it does not establish a cause-and-effect relationship between exercise and smoking cessation. Perhaps the most accurate conclusion at this time is that exercise offers another option for cigarette smokers who have inclinations to become non-smokers. The bottom line may be that if one is truly committed to quitting, one will succeed in spite of the method, but if the resolve is weak, one will fail regardless of the method. Exercise is a viable and valid option because the benefits received from physical activity cannot be maximized while continuing to smoke. Many smokers who become hooked on the exercise and fitness habit become unhooked from the smoking habit.

Obesity

According to deVries, "There are very few, very fat, very old people around. Your own observations and the national statistics — clearly show that long life does not mean survival of the fattest."[19] Morbidity (the sick rate or ratio of sick to well in a population) and mortality (the death rate or ratio of actual to expected deaths in a population) are greater among the obese than among those of normal weight. Men who are 30 percent above desirable weight experience 70 percent greater mortality than men of normal weight.[20]

Obesity is gender-linked; that is, it is defined as more than 23 percent body fat for men and more and 30 percent for women.[21] Overweight may be defined as excessive weight for one's height with no regard for its composition. In the context of this book, this term is useless for counseling people about weight loss. For example, a very muscular male, who is 6'1" tall with only 10 percent body fat, may weigh 230 pounds. According to the new height/weight charts, he is considerably overweight, but his low percentage of body fat indicates that he is carrying a significant amount of muscle tissue. It would be very difficult for this man to lose weight and remain healthy. On the other hand, a sedentary male of the same height who weighs 190 pounds, 24 percent of which is in the form of fat, is not overweight but definitely overfat. This individual falls in the obese range and should be counseled to lose fat tissue while maintaining or building muscle tissue.

The risk of obesity as an independent factor in heart disease is difficult to evaluate. Under any circumstance, ". . . extreme obesity is clearly detrimental to health and longevity, while lesser degrees of overweight worsen the prevalent conditions — high blood pressure and diabetes — and predispose to gallstones."[22] Uncomplicated mild overfatness (accompanied by no other risk factors) probably represents little risk. But obesity generally coexists with other factors and combines with them to increase and complicate the risk. A national study of one million subjects showed a consistent and strongly positive relationship between obesity and hypertension.[23] Approximately 53 to 80 percent of the adult-onset diabetics (Type II) are obese.[24] Low back problems are aggravated by obesity because the further out a "potbelly" protrudes, the more force it exerts upon the back.[25] In addition, obesity increases the risk of, or exacerbates, stroke, osteoarthritis, cirrhosis of the liver, pregnancy, likelihood of accidents, and surgery, to name but a few.[26]

Weight gain generally occurs imperceptibly, or so it seems, over many years. We tend to tolerate it to a certain point or threshold. Crossing the threshold produces dissatisfaction with our appearance and energizes us to map out a strategy aimed at regaining our once-streamlined silhouette. When motivated into action people generally respond by dieting, which means changing eating habits for a period of time until the target weight or a compromise target has been achieved. Most people can successfully lose weight by dieting but they usually find that the accomplishment is temporary as the lost weight is eventually regained — often with a bit more. The often-neglected factor in a weight loss program is exercise. Exercise and diet are not mutually exclusive; they are complementary, with each having a contribution to make. The role of exercise was addressed at an international meeting on obesity in 1983 and the unanimous consensus of the experts was: "if you are about to start a weight reduction program or if you're trying to maintain your present weight, success or failure can depend on whether or not you exercise.[27]

Diabetes Mellitus

Diabetes mellitus is a metabolic disorder which is characterized by an insulin deficiency. Insulin is a hormone produced by the pancreas which is needed to transport sugar into the body's cells. It does this by binding to insulin receptors on the surfaces of target cells thus stimulating the channels to open up and receive sugar (glucose).

Type I diabetes is a genetic disorder which usually occurs prior to the age of 10. Victims generally produce no insulin so they take it by injection. Although this has been a significant achievement in the treatment of diabetes, insulin taken by injection is not the same physiologically as that which is produced and secreted naturally by the pancreas. For example, the pancreas of a nondiabetic automatically monitors blood sugar levels and secretes insulin when it is needed (after a meal) and reduces its secretion when less is needed (during exercise). Insulin-dependent diabetics do not have the luxury of this exquisitely balanced system but instead they inject insulin all at once. Even if a diabetic is living a well-regulated life, occasional imbalances occur between glucose levels and insulin. This results in a lag time between the need for insulin and its availability and contributes to premature deterioration of the cardiovascular system.

Type II diabetes usually occurs after 40 years of age to sedentary overweight people. Eighty percent of all diabetes is of the Type II variety. This type of diabetes is characterized by the production of more than enough insulin but an inadequate number of insulin receptors. As a result, target cells are unable to receive glucose so its level in the blood rises. As Type II diabetes progresses, some people will also produce insufficient quantities of insulin. Treatment includes hypoglycemic (sugar lowering) drugs, a low-fat diet, exercise, and weight control. Management of Type II diabetes without drugs is the preferred strategy and for most diabetics it is an achievable goal. Oral hypoglycemic drugs promote the accumulation of fat, making weight loss a difficult proposition. Excessive weight increases the cell's resistance to insulin, increasing dependence upon the hypoglycemic drugs, which in turn inhibits weight loss, and the proverbial vicious cycle becomes firmly established. Exercise and weight loss, however, combine to increase the number of insulin receptors while simultaneously enhancing their sensitivity to insulin. The net result is that more glucose can enter more cells more quickly.[28]

Diabetes cannot be cured but it can be controlled, which is the key to living a long and productive life. Depending upon the type of diabetes, control involves some combination of injectable insulin, oral hypoglycemic agents, meal planning, exercise, and weight loss. Jogging reduces the need for insulin, decreases blood platelet adhesiveness for about 24 hours, and ameliorates the severity of the cardiovascular risk factors.

Stress

It is estimated that 50 to 75 percent of all people who visit a physician do so for psychosomatic disorders. These are illnesses that orginate in the mind and manifest themselves in physical ailments. Since the mind and body function in unison, can we accomplish the reverse? Can we strengthen the body (heart, circulatory, respiratory, muscular systems, etc.) and produce a positive effect upon the mind? According to Cooper, the answer from both theory and research is "yes."[29]

The psychological and emotional benefits of endurance-type exercise — which are difficult to quantify — are just beginning to be understood. This area of research became more promising when several types of opiate-like brain chemicals that were reputed to produce elevations in mood, feelings of tranquility, and increased tolerance to pain were identified in the early 1970s. We will concentrate only upon one of these chemicals, the beta endorphins, because they have been more extensively researched and because their effects may be more pronounced. This field of study is not without problems. The endorphins are difficult to measure and many of the tools and techniques used in their assessment are relatively crude. Also, these substances are commonly measured in the blood but their pharmacological effect occurs in the brain. Endorphin elevations in the blood may not necessarily translate into endorphin elevations in the brain due to blood-brain barriers that might not allow the endorphins to filter through.

Jogging seems to elevate the level of endorphins in the blood. Most of the studies have used jogging as the activity of choice and a majority of these have shown increases in circulating endorphins. At this point, the conclusions regarding the relationship between exercise and the endorphins are not set in concrete. Further study and more sophisticated techniques will eventually clarify the function of endorphins as well as the effect of exercise upon their production.

Jogging has been used successfully as therapy for relieving anxiety and mental depression.[30] Scientists who are presently trying to unravel the mysteries associated with the emotional effects of exercise have more questions than answers. But the people who have been exercising consistently voice their opinions unreservedly. They report feeling more relaxed, sleeping more soundly, having more energy, and feeling better than at any other time in their lives. To them, these are the important benefits; how and why they occur are of little consequence.

The average participant is not concerned with whether the effect is elicited from the endorphins, or the feeling of well-being associated with exercise, or the feeling of taking charge of this aspect of their lives, or some other reason that has yet to be identified. The important factor is that these effects occur, and the feelings expressed by faithful exercisers are genuine and, in their perceptions, are tied in a causal way to their exercise program.

Too many people report similar experiences for it to be coincidental. In time, scientists will resolve the whys and how, but for now we should place some deserved emphasis upon the subjective feelings connected with physical activity. We can predict that these will occur in an appropriately planned and executed exercise program.

Physical Inactivity

Physical inactivity (hypokinesis) has a debilitating effect upon the human body. A few weeks of bed rest results in muscle atrophy, bone demineralization, and decreases in cardiovascular endurance and maximum respiratory capacity.[31] The old adage "use or lose it" was demonstrated by this study.

A recent review of literature by researchers at the Centers for Disease Control indicated that physical inactivity seems to be causally related with coronary heart disease.[32] Sedentary people are 1.9 times more likely to develop coronary heart disease than people who exercise for 20 minutes, three times per week.[33] These researchers concluded that

> High systolic blood pressure, high serum cholesterol, cigarette smoking, and physical inactivity — have similar relative risks. But there are far more people who fail to perform regular physical activity than people who have systolic blood pressure equal to or greater than 150, have serum cholesterol equal to or greater than 268 mg/100ml, or smoke one pack or more of cigarettes per day. Thus it is likely that increasing levels of physical activity in the population at large may have more effect on lowering levels of coronary heart disease than would modifying any one of the other risk factors.

Paffenbarger's long-term investigation of Harvard Alumni, aged 35-74, showed that physical activity was positively related to length of life.[34] The death rates among alumni decreased as their energy expenditure increased in such activities as walking, stair climbing and sports play. Death rates were 25 to 33 percent lower among those who expended 2000 kcals or more per week when compared to the less active alumni. This relationship held regardless of whether the subjects were hypertensive, cigarette smokers, overweight or had a family history of premature death. The active alumni lived approximately two years longer than their sedentary peers.

An eight and one-half year study of 3106 men aged 30-69 showed that level of fitness influenced the risk of death.[35] Men with the highest fitness level, as determined by a maximum exercise tolerance test, were three times less likely to die of a heart attack during the 8½ year follow-up. These data emerged after being adjusted for age, smoking, blood pressure and serum cholesterol.

Jogging and other vigorous forms of exercise are not without their critics. The spectrum of criticism generally includes susceptibility to musculoskeletal injuries, early onset of arthritis and sudden death from heart attack. While it is true that physical activity stresses the body, it is through this stress that the body becomes stronger. Musculoskeletal injuries will occur even when one trains intelligently but they should not occur frequently. The early onset of arthritis will be dealt with in the next section.

How many jogging-related deaths are the result of chance rather than exercise? When people die under these circumstances, the immediate inference is that the death was caused by jogging because that is what the person was doing at the time. The hypothesis would seem to be that if middle-aged and older adults would abstain from jogging, these premature deaths could be avoided. If we expand upon this ostensibly logical but naive reasoning, we would also have to abstain from sleeping or driving or watching TV because many more heart attacks occur during these activities than from jogging.

Obviously, establishing cause and effect is elusive because the atherosclerotic process takes years to culminate in a heart attack. What the individual was doing at the time, except in certain circumstances, probably had little bearing on the result.

The expected level of cardiovascular deaths on the basis of chance alone while runners are running has been investigated.[36] Data from the National Center of Health Statistics indicated that 100 cardiovascular deaths per year among runners in the U.S. could be expected purely on the basis of time. But the number of reported jogging-related deaths is considerably below this number. This research dispels the general notion that jogging is unsafe.

The results of an important long-awaited community based study by Siscovick and his group that examined the relationship between vigorous exercise and the risk of sudden cardiac death was reported in the New England Journal of Medicine.[37] The researchers' approach was unique because they examined concurrently the potential risk of sudden cardiac death during vigorous exercise and the potential benefits associated with habitual exercise in the same population. According to their data, sedentary men who engage in vigorous exercise less than 20 minutes per week are three times more likely to die suddenly than men who exercise vigorously more than two hours and twenty minutes per week. Although the active men have a slightly elevated risk of sudden death during exercise, the long-term health benefits clearly outweigh the mortality risk when compared to the sedentary men. The risk of sudden death during exercise for sedentary men was 56 times greater than their risk at other times. Active men have a mortality advantage at rest and during exercise when compared to sedentary men.

OSTEOPOROSIS

Osteoporosis, which literally means porous bone, is a degenerative disease which follows a long insidious course usually beginning about age 35 for females and 55 for males. The bones gradually lose their mineral content and tensile strength rendering them more susceptible to breaking. Particularly affected are the bones of the spinal column, wrist, and hip. A hip fracture is potentially life threatening for an older individual. Osteoporosis is responsible for approximately 227,000 hip fractures[38] and an estimated 30,000 deaths.[39]

Osteoporosis is a multi-factorial disease; that is, it is affected by several factors including calcium and fluoride deficiencies, reduction in the production of estrogen, and lack of exercise. At highest risk are those who are female, white or Oriental, have a slender body type, and experience early menopause.[38]

Calcium supplementation tends to help those who are calcium deficient and whose disease is the result of this deficiency.[40] Osteoporosis can be experimentally induced in laboratory animals by limiting calcium intake. This process can be reversed by supplying adequate amounts of calcium in the diet. It is becoming increasingly clear that estrogen replacement in women who are deficient in this hormone will arrest and possibly reverse osteoporosis.[41] The fluoride effect on osteoporosis remains equivocal[42] however, it appears that fluoride therapy is associated with the formation of new bony tissue and that bone mass is increased in the axial skeleton (spinal column, ribs, breastbone, and skull).

Physical activity and lack of physical activity have opposite effects. For example, bed rest results in significant demineralization of bone. It appears that muscular contractions and gravitational forces which are applied while the individual is in an upright position are necessary and/or build new bony tissue.[43] Many studies which have compared active and inactive people and athletes and non-athletes have shown that the active groups and athletes have thicker, heavier bones.[44, 45] Bone mineral content was increased in the used arm of baseball and tennis players when compared to their non-used arm.[46, 47] The stresses imposed on muscles and bones with vigorous activity leads to hypertrophy of both tissues. Weight bearing activities such as walking, jogging, rope jumping, etc. seem to be better suited to maintaining and developing bony tissue than non-weight bearing activities such as swimming and cycling.

SUMMARY

Many of the risk factors associated with chronic disease and early death may be modified negatively or positively by the way we live. The blood fats, cholesterol and triglycerides, blood pressure, obesity, diabetes, physical inactivity, stress, tension and anxiety can be changed for the better through healthy dietary and exercise patterns. Millions have given up smoking and millions have rediscovered the pleasure, as well as the health-related benefits of regular exercise. Living habits influence the quality and the quantity of life. Exercise is one of the positive factors which requires effort and commitment — but the rewards are well worth the effort. We ultimately are responsible for our actions and we reap the benefits or pay the price accordingly.

REFERENCES

1. *Heart Facts,* American Heart Association, 1978.
2. Keil, J. E. and others. "Hypertension: Effects of Social Class and Racial Admixture," *American Journal of Public Health,* 67:634, 1977.
3. Chesler, E. and others. "Myocardial Infarction In The Black Population of South Africa: Coronary Angiographic Finding," *American Heart Journal,* 95:691, 1978.
4. Yano, K. and others. "Dietary Intake and the Risk of Coronary Heart Disease in Japanese Men Living in Hawaii," *American Journal of Clinical Nutrition,* 31:1270, 1978.
5. Robertson, T. L. and others. "Epidemiologic Studies of Coronary Heart Disease in Japanese Men Living in Hawaii and California," *American Journal of Cardiology,* 39:239, 1977.
6. "Cholesterol Testing: The Numbers Game," *University of California, Berkely Wellness Letter,* 3: Issue 9, 5, June, 1987.
7. Sheenan, G. "George Sheehan's Viewpoint," *Runner's World,* 14, July, 1987.
8. Williams, P. T. and others. "The Effect of Running Mileage and Duration on Plasma Lipoprotein Levels," *Journal of the American Medical Association,* 247:No. 19, 2674, May 21, 1982.
9. Hamilton, E. M. N. and Whitney, E. N. *Nutrition Concepts and Controversies,* St. Paul, Mn: West Publishing Co., 1982.
10. Cullinaria, E. and others. "Acute Decrease In Serum Triglycerides With Exercise: Is There a Threshold for an Exercise Effect?," *Metabolism,* 31:844, 1982.
11. Boyer, J. and Kasch, F. "Exercise Therapy," 1668; Kilborn, A. and others. "Physical Training in Sedentary Middle-Aged and Older Men," *Scandinavian Journal of Clinical Laboratory Investigation,* 24:315, 1969.
12. de Vries, H. A. Physiological Effects of an Exercise Training Regimen Upon Men Aged 52-85," *Journal of Gerontology,* 25:325, 1970.
13. Fletcher, G. F. *Exercise in the Practice of Medicine,* New York: Futura Publishing Co., 1982.
14. Lamb, L. (ed.) "Your Vital Blood Pressure," *The Health Letter,* 15, No. 8: April 25, 1980.
15. "1983 Surgeon General's Report Health Consequences of Smoking," *Smoking and Health Reporter,* 1 no. 2: 1, January, 1984.
16. *Cancer Facts and Figures for 1984,* New York: American Cancer Society, 1984.
17. Wilmore, J. H. "Exercise: The Aerobic Edge," *Food and Fitness,* The First International Videoconference on Good Eating, Exercise and Health, 47, March 30, 1984.
18. "Running — Ups and Downs" *Harvard Medical School Health Letter,* 5, May, 1983.
19. de Vries, H. A. *Health Science,* Santa Monica, Ca.: Goodyear Publishing Co., 1979.
20. Katch, F. I. and McArdle, W. D. *Nutrition, Weight Control, and Exercise,* Philadelphia: Lea and Febiger, 1983.
21. Howley, E. T. and Franks, B. D. *Health/Fitness Instructor's Handbook,* Champaign, Ill: Human Kinetics Publishers, Inc., 1986.
22. Wood, P. D. "The Science of Successful Weight Loss" *Food and Fitness,* First International Videoconference On Good Eating, Exercise, and Health, 3, March 30, 1984.
23. Stamler, R. and others. "Weight and Blood Pressure: Findings In Hypertension Screening of One

Million Americans," *Journal of the American Medical Association,* 240:1607, 1978.

24. *Competitive Problems in the Drug Industry — Oral Hypoglycemic Drugs,* Washington: U.S. Government Printing Office, 1975.

25. Day, N. R. *Back to Backs,* Daly City, Ca.: Krames Communications, 1983.

26. Marley, W. P. *Health and Physical Fitness,* New York: Saunders College Publishing, 1982.

27. Stern, J. S. "Movement Makes the Difference" *Food and Fitness,* The First International Videoconference On Good Eating, Exercise, and Health, 49, March 30, 1984.

28. Day, N. R. *Controlling Type II Diabetes,* Daly City, Ca.: Krames Communications, 1983.

29. Cooper, K. H. *The Aerobic Way,* New York: Bantam Books, 1977.

30. Brown, R. J. and others, "The Prescription of Exercise for Depression," *The Physician and Sportsmedicine,* 6:35, December, 1978.

31. Saltin, B. and others, "Response to Exercise After Bed Rest and After Training," *Circulation Supplement* 1:7, 1968.

32. Powell, K. E. and others. "Physical Activity and the Incidence of Coronary Heart Disease," *Annual Review of Public Health,* 8:253, 1987.

33. Caspersen, C. J. "Physical Inactivity and Coronary Heart Disease," *The Physician and Sportsmedicine,* 15, No. 11: 43, November, 1987.

34. Paffenbarger, R. S. and others. "Physical Activity, All-Cause Mortality, and Longevity of College Alumni," *The New England Medical Journal,* 314, No. 10:605, March 6, 1986.

35. Kirk, B. "Fitness Influences Risk of Death," *April Medical Journal,* 52:3, April, 1987.

36. Kaplan, J. P. "Cardiovascular Deaths While Running," *Journal of the American Medical Association,* 242:2578, 1979.

37. Siscovick, D. S. and others. "The Incidence of Primary Cardiac Arrest During Vigorous Exercise," *The New England Journal of Medicine,* 311:874, October 4, 1984.

38. "Milk Helps Ward Off Osteoporosis," *Tufts University Diet and Nutrition Letter,* 3, No. 11:2, January, 1986.

39. Johnston, C. E. and Slemonda, C. "Osteoporosis: An Overview," *The Physician and Sportsmedicine,* 15, No. 11:65, November, 1987.

40. Heaney, R. P. "The Role of Calcium in Prevention and Treatment of Osteoporosis," *The Physician and Sportsmedicine,* 15, No. 11:83, November, 1987.

41. Lindsay, R. L. "Estrogen and Osteoporosis," *The Physician and Sportsmedicine,* 15, No. 11:105, November, 1987.

42. Hedlund, L. R. and Gallagher, J. C. "The Effect of Fluoride in Osteoporosis," *The Physician and Sportsmedicine,* 15, No. 11:111, November, 1987.

43. Smith, E. L. and Gilligen, C. "Effects of Inactivity and Exercise on Bone," *The Physician and Sportsmedicine,* 15, No. 11:91, November, 1987.

44. Brewer, V. and others. "Role of Exercise in Prevention of Involutional Bone Loss," *Medicine and Science in Sports and Exercise,* 15, No. 6:445, 1983.

45. Lane, N. E. and others. "Long-Distance Running, Bone Density, and Osteoporosis," *Journal of the American Medical Association,* 255, No. 9:1147, March 7, 1986.

46. Jones, H. H. and others. "Humeral Hypertrophy in Response to Exercise," *Journal of Bone and Joint Surgery,* 59:204, March, 1977.

47. Montoye, H. J. and others. "Bone Mineral in Senior Tennis Players," *Scandinavian Journal of Sports Sciences,* 2, No. 1:26, 1980.

CHAPTER SIX

Motivation

BASICS OF MOTIVATION

Motivation is a label invented by people to describe a characteristic type of behavior. It cannot be measured directly; therefore it is inferred through observations of behaviors and actions. Such imprecision often results in inaccurate perceptions about presumed levels of motivation. The matter is confused further because motivation, as with other aspects of human behavior, lacks a uniformly acceptable definition. For this text, we will adopt Sage's definition that motivation is "the internal mechanisms and external stimuli that arouse and direct behavior."[1] According to this definition, motivation is affected by both internal and external forces.

External forces, represented by extrinsic (external) rewards, often are a necessary stimulus for people to continue jogging during those critical early months. For instance, membership in an exercise group provides a setting where compliments and positive strokes from one's peers furnish the external reinforcement for adherence during this time. Franklin stated, "the benefits derived from extrinsic rewards, while initially important, are also short-lived. Ultimately, the motivation to continue an exercise program must be intrinsic rather than extrinsic in nature. The individual must develop an attitude toward exercise which reinforces adherence."[2] Buffington stated that each individual is his or her own best motivator, as the greatest motivational energy comes from within.[3] The drive producing long-term adherence in any endeavor, exercise included, must be intrinsically motivated.

Human behavior is purposeful; that is, it is goal-directed. The objective of motivated behavior is the achievement of our goals. Positive reinforcements (intrinsic supplemented with extrinsic) motivate us to persist in the attainment of these goals. A workable plan for achieving goals involves knowing what we want to accomplish in the long run. In other words, we should be able to identify our long-range goals. Then we should set realistic short-term goals which may be reached within a reasonable time. The achievement of each short-term goal acts as both a reinforcer and a stimulus motivating us to strive for the next goal, while each accomplishment brings us closer to realizing our long-term goal. The key is realism: setting goals that are difficult enough to provide a challenge but that we have a reasonable chance of achieving. This is a feasible way to approach your fitness goals.

Some psychologists have determined that a moderate level of motivation is optimal. Too little is likely to result in early failure and too much may result in injury and burnout. In either case, motivation is adversely affected, adherence wanes, and the program, with all its good intentions and potential benefits, is terminated. In order to avert this all-too-familiar scenario, we must cultivate the philosophy that our fitness goals should be approached slowly and patiently, albeit progressively. We must learn to contain our enthusiasm so as not to attempt too much too soon during the early phases of the program. Remember, physical fitness is not achieved with two weeks of training. The development and maintenance of physical fitness should be a life-long affair. This requires a sizeable commitment of time and knowledgeable effort, but the results are eminently worthwhile. You supply the time and the effort and this text will provide you with the necessary knowledge. The appropriate application of these ingredients will increase your likelihood of success.

Factors which are motivating to one person may not have the same effect upon another due to differences in experience, interests, aims, objectives, intelligence, etc.; therefore, selection of the exact factor or factors which will motivate any given individual to participate in a long-term jogging program is conjectural at best. Most people become involved with exercise for health-related reasons.[4] These include weight loss, reduction of stress and anxiety, prevention or delay of heart disease, strengthening the musculoskeletal systems, desire to live better and longer, and to sleep more restfully. The original reason for participation often becomes the primary reinforcer for maintaining the program. In some instances the original reason is blended with others or assumes lesser importance as progress occurs. But in far too many cases, slightly more than fifty percent of the participants discontinue the program. The failure rate would undoubtedly be less if more was known about the techniques of motivation. For compliance to remain high, the motive for participation must eventually be internalized. As Franklin said, "The individual must develop an attitude toward exercise which reinforces adherence."[2]

Unfortunately, being knowledgeable about the beneficial health effects of exercise is usually not enough of a motivator for many people. Most people know that exercise is good for health enhancement yet many don't participate. Having some knowledge simply is not enough to stimulate people to make positive lifestyle behavioral changes. Millions of people know that smoking cigarettes is harmful to their health yet they continue to smoke. Likewise, millions of people know that exercise is good for them yet they continue to lead sedentary lives.

It is difficult to determine which event or set of circumstances will motivate a given individual. We have at our disposal a variety of techniques which may enhance exercise continuance. These help, in a general way, to maintain the enthusiasm for a physically active life. However, predicting the precise motive which will stimulate a specific individual to exercise remains elusive. The following strategies may help.

SOME MOTIVATIONAL STRATEGIES

Develpment of a Knowledge Base

Understanding the need for exercise as well as the associated health-related benefits may be a sufficient stimulus for some people to act but it is inadequate for the majority of sedentary individuals. However, Ken Cooper's first book motivated millions of sedentary Americans to become physically active. Knowledge provides a rationale for an active life, and for those who respond positively to cognitive information, it may be a primary motivator. As such, it should not be deleted from the techniques which are commonly employed to enhance exercise adherence.

Set Realistic Goals

Set realistic and attainable goals. Don't expect too much too soon. Be patient because fitness takes time. At the same time, don't become excessively goal-oriented. Remain flexible and change your goals if and when the need occurs.

Do not go beyond your capacity by raising the intensity level too abruptly. This will most assuredly lead to discomfort and to possible injury. In either case, the program will probably be terminated. One study has shown that the injury rate rises when the jogger participates more than five days per week for more than 45 minutes per session.[5]

Beginners should jog every other day and limit the duration of each workout to 20 to 30 minutes exclusive of warm-up and cool-down. As fitness improves the length and frequency of jogging can be increased in a manner consistent with the attainment of your goals. Monitor your heart rate and keep the degree of exertion between 70-85 percent of the maximal heart rate. Remember that people differ genetically in their potential for aerobic activity. We cannot all achieve the same level of performance, but we all can improve our aerobic capacity.

Jog With A Group

Two investigators compared Cooper's individualized aerobics program[6] to the group approach and found that after 28 weeks only 47 percent of those in the individualized program continued to participate compared to 82 percent in the group system.[7] An attractive feature of group participation is the possibility of developing social relationships with other participants.[8] The group provides reinforcement, camaraderie, and an element of competition as well as a spirit of cooperation. In the early days of exercise, allegiance to a group enhances compliance; one's commitment to the group is not as easily dissolved as a commitment to oneself. When the individual becomes committed to regular participation in exercise, the need for group support will probably decrease and the program can be continued without it.

The "buddy-support" system represents another technique for continued participation.[9, 10] These researchers indicated that this model might provide the necessary support for sustaining an exercise program. Two people with similar training routines and compatible levels of fitness can reinforce each other. Knowing that your training buddy will be waiting for you at a designated time and place makes it difficult to skip the workout even when you would rather do something else. Associate with people who motivate you in a positive manner and avoid those who are negative and pessimistic. Don't allow them to give you a negative attitude. Seek out others who exercise and, with them, discuss training, nutrition, weight loss, the reasons why they began exercising, what they have already accomplished, what you hope to do and then learn from each other. Catch their enthusiasm and give them some of yours. Enthusiasm is prevalent and contagious when people who exercise get together; as a result of this interaction you will eagerly approach your next workout.

Enlist the Aid of Significant Others

Spouses, family members, friends, and co-workers, those with whom the individual interacts frequently, can be primary sources of support. In one study, 80 percent of the husbands whose wives had a positive attitude toward their exercise program exhibited good to excellent adherence while only 40 percent of those men whose wives had negative or neutral attitudes were in these categories.[11] This indicates that some effort should be made by the prospective jogger to enlist the support of significant others. Sharing knowledge about the potential benefits as well as aims and objectives for embarking upon a jogging program may create a positive and supportive attitude among those people who are important to the jogger.

Keep A Progress Chart

It is sometimes helpful to keep a daily record because this written information objectively shows the rate and amount of progress which has been achieved. Looking back at the record and observing the gains that have been made can be a source of motivation when one becomes discouraged. The chart should reflect changes in body weight, type and amount of exercise, duration, and the exercising and resting heart rates. There should also be room for a short accompanying statement on how the participant felt during and after the workout. See Appendix C.

Weighing oneself prior to and after the workout is important particularly in hot weather when fluid loss can become a major problem. Most of the weight lost during the workout is liquid so the difference between pre- and post-exercise weight is an approximation of the amount of fluid loss. This figure should not exceed four to five percent of the body's weight. This process of determining and/or approximating fluid loss is one of the functional aspects of the progress chart. Over the long term, a trend for weight loss, distance covered, and heart rates (exercise and resting) will become discernible and you will have a record of improvement.

Jog To Music

Music provides a sense of rhythm and it tends to take one's mind off the effort associated with jogging. A researcher at Ohio State University tested experienced runners with and without up-beat music.[12] The runners stated that music made the bout of exercise seem easier. They ran both trials, one with and one without music, at the same workload. Measures of working heart rates and blood lactate indicated that the runners were working equally hard on both trials, only their perceptions of the difficulty of the workload were changed. Music can be easily provided indoors and portable radio headsets are gaining in popularity for outdoor running.

Set A Definite Time And Place For Jogging

It is best to set a definite time and locate a convenient place during the initial stages of the exercise program. Resolve to jog at least three times per week and schedule your workout as you would any other important activity. Resist the temptation to replace your workout with some other pursuit that might be more appealing. Skipping workouts becomes habit-forming; the more you do it the easier it becomes. After you become hooked on exercise (it takes three to six months), the time and/or place may be varied to meet the vagaries of weather, job responsibilities, and aesthetic sensibilities.

When is the best time of day to work out? This is an often asked question. In the past, I would answer by saying that the time of day that fits best into a busy schedule is the best time to exercise. This is still valid but here are a couple of other considerations. The best time of day to jog might be immediately at the end of the work day and before supper. This should serve two purposes: (1) it will metabolize the stress products which have accumulated in the blood during the day, and (2) it will temporarily suppress the appetite resulting in the consumption of fewer calories at supper.

With regard to exercise and weight loss, there is some evidence which supports the notion that the best time of day to exercise is before breakfast. A study at Kent State, which was reported in the *Daily Pulse* (a newsletter of Methodist Hospitals of Memphis) indicated that an early morning jog burned more fat calories than an after-lunch jog.[13] The researcher tested a group of runners after a 12 hour fast before breakfast and then tested the same group after a 3 to 4 hour fast after lunch. The group ran for 30 minutes each time and burned the same number of calories each time, but two-thirds of the calories expended in the before-breakfast jog were fat while only 50 percent of the after lunch jog calories were fat. The before-breakfast jog comes after a night of sleep, which represents the longest period of time that most people go without food or beverages. The extra fat burned in exercise in the morning may be due to low pre-breakfast insulin levels. Insulin encourages carbohydrate use and inhibits the use of fat, therefore exercise which occurs when blood insulin is low causes a shift to greater reliance upon fat as a fuel.

SUMMARY

Motivation describes a characteristic type of behavior. It cannot be measured directly, instead it is inferred through observation of behaviors and actions and therefore, can lead to errors of assessment. The specific stimulus which will motivate a given individual to begin jogging cannot accurately be predicted, but in general terms it is quite well known that most people exercise for health-related reasons. But there are some techniques which tend to improve exercise compliance. These include learning the basics of how and why of exercise, setting realistic goals, jogging with a buddy or a group, having the support of people who are important in your life, keeping a progress chart, using music which tends to decrease the perception of effort, and in the beginning, setting a definite time and place for exercise.

REFERENCES

1. Sage, G. *Motor Learning and Control: A Neurophysiological Approach*, Dubuque, Iowa: William C. Brown Publishers, 1984.
2. Franklin, B. A. "Motivating and Educating Adults to Exercise," *Journal of Physical Education and Recreation*, 49, No. 6:6, 1978.
3. Buffington, J. H. "Getting Going," *Sky* 112, April, 1985.
4. Harris, G. and Kagan, J. "The Fitness Advantage" *American Health*, 4, No. 5:12, June, 1985.
5. Pollock, M. L. and others. "Effects of Frequency and Duration of Training on Attrition and Incidence of Injury," *Medicine and Science in Sports*, 9:31, 1977.
6. Cooper, K. *The Aerobics Way*, New York: Bantam Books, 1977.
7. Massie, J. F. and Shephard, R. J. "Physiological and Psychological Effects of Training — A Comparison of Individual and Gymnasium Programs With a Characterization of Exercise Drop-Out," *Medicine and Science in Sports*, 3:110, 1971.
8. Massie, J. F. and Shephard, R. J. "Physiological and Psychological Effects of Training," *Fitness Ontario: Those Who Know But Don't Do*, Toronto, Ontario: Ministry of Culture and Recreation, 1981.
9. Wankel, L. M. "Motivating Involvement in Adult Physical Activity Programs," *Recreation Research Review*, 6:40, 1979.
10. Wanzel, R. S. "Toward Preventing Dropouts in Industrial and Other Fitness Programmes," *Recreation Canada*, 36:39, 1978.
11. Heinzelmann, F. and Bagley, R. "Response to Physical Activity Programs and Their Effect On Health Behavior," *Public Health Reports*, 85:905, 1970.
12. Trotter, R. J. "Maybe It's the Music," *Psychology Today*, 8, May, 1984.
13. "Wake-Up Workouts," *Daily Pulse*, 5, No. 3:4, January/February, 1987.

CHAPTER SEVEN

Prevention and Treatment of Common Jogging Injuries

GENERAL PRINCIPLES OF PREVENTION

The often-heard adage, "an ounce of prevention is worth a pound of cure" is applicable when one embarks upon a jogging program. It continues to be appropriate advice even for seasoned joggers because after an injury-free period some of them become complacent and disregard the principles which have contributed to the avoidance of injury. The best way to deal with jogging injuries is to prevent their occurrence. Previous chapters have focused upon the principles of training which are designed to promote aerobic fitness with maximum safety. Briefly, some of these are:

1. Contain your enthusiasm. Enthusiasm is necessary for success, but too much may lead to overexertion and injury. Increasing the distance or decreasing the time required to cover a given distance should occur slowly and progressively.
2. Those with multiple risks or those over 45 years of age should obtain clearance for jogging by a physician.
3. The program should be individualized to meet the jogger's aims and objectives.
4. The exercise intensity of each workout should not exceed 85 percent of maximal heart rate.

5. The duration of each workout should be within the 20 to 30 minute range in the early stages of the program and be lengthened as fitness improves.
6. In the beginning, jog every other day and increase the frequency to a level which is consistent with physical improvement and program objectives.
7. Wear quality jogging shoes.
8. Adjust the intensity and duration of the workout according to the environmental conditions.
9. Hydrate fully prior to the workout, continue to drink liquid during and after the workout.
10. Follow sound warm-up and cool-down procedures.
11. Work to improve jogging form.
12. Choose running surfaces which are less likely to promote injury.

TREATMENT AND PREVENTION OF SELECTED JOGGING INJURIES

Prospective joggers should take the necessary precautions to prevent injuries. Should one occur, proper and immediate treatment can minimize its severity and the attendant length of inactivity. Several studies have shown that the number of miles jogged per week is the most significant factor associated with the probability of developing an injury.[1]

Chafing

Chafing usually occurs in areas where there is a high degree of friction. For example, people with large thighs that rub together will experience chafing. This is a minor but aggravating injury which can easily be prevented by applying a generous coat of vaseline to susceptible areas prior to the workout. Treatment for chafing is immediate cessation of jogging with the onset of irritation and application of an antiseptic lotion.

Blisters

Blisters are painful friction burns of a minor nature which result in fluid filled sacs of various sizes. Blisters may be prevented by wearing properly fitted shoes, clean socks, and employing the correct footstrike. Additionally, foot or talcum powder may be sprinkled inside socks and shoes to reduce friction.

Apply moleskin (toughskin) to those areas of the feet where there is a higher tendency to form blisters. "Hot spots" are reddened areas which will become blisters very quickly if preventive measures are not taken. Should a blister form, wash the area thoroughly with soap and water and apply a generous coat of iodine to it and the surrounding area. Then use a sterile needle to puncture the blister at its base and squeeze out the accumulated fluid. When this is completed, apply an antiseptic medication and a sterile dressing. Jogging may be continued after treatment by cutting a doughnut from foam rubber and taping it over the blister.

Muscle Soreness

Muscle soreness subsequent to jogging is probably due to microscopic tears in muscle fibers and damage to muscle membranes.[3] This damage is partially responsible for the localized pain, tenderness and swelling experienced by the jogger 24 to 72 hours after the workout.[4] Downhill running has been implicated in delayed muscle soreness. In downhill running, the leg muscles contract eccentrically, that is, they produce force as they lengthen. Running uphill produces the opposite effect as the muscles contract concentrically to provide the lift needed to negotiate the upgrade. To further expand upon this concept, when a weight is lifted, the muscles contract concentrically to produce the force needed to raise the weight against the force of gravity. When the weight is set down, the muscles contract eccentrically, lengthen, and produce the same amount of force to slow its descent. It is this portion of the movement that results in delayed muscle soreness. In a simple yet ingenious study, Newham and others had their subjects exercise by consistently stepping onto a box with one leg and stepping down with the other.[5] The step-up represented the concentric contraction and the step down was the eccentric contraction. The subjects experienced pain which peaked 48 hours after the exercise in the eccentrically exercised leg only.

The delayed soreness experienced with eccentric exercise is probably due to the recruitment of only a few muscle fibers which must produce great tension to perform the work. Untrained people experience greater delayed muscle soreness than trained people.

Delayed muscle soreness may be prevented by keeping the intensity, duration and frequency of exercise within one's ability level, by progressing slowly, by doing daily stretching exercises and by jogging on a flat surface in the initial stages of training. As one becomes more fit, uphill and downhill running should be carefully included in the routine. If soreness occurs, it should be treated with rest as well as stretching the affected muscles several times per day.

Muscle Cramps

Muscle cramps are sudden, powerful, involuntary muscle contractions which produce considerable pain. Some cramps are recurrent, that is, they are characterized by repeated contractions and relaxation of the muscles, while others produce steady continuous contraction. Preventive measures include a gradual warm-up which includes stretching exercises. Overfatigue should be avoided.

Causes associated with muscle cramping are difficult to establish. Fatigue, depletion of both body fluids and minerals, and loss of muscle coordination have all been implicated to some extent.

Muscle cramps should not be massaged because there may be underlying blood vessel damage and internal bleeding. Vigorous massage in this case would aggravate the condition and promote additional damage. Treatment should include firm, consistent pressure at the site of the cramp. This should be followed by the application of ice and then the affected muscle should be stretched.

Achilles Tendon Injuries

The achilles tendon connects the calf muscle to the heel of the foot. Achilles tendonitis is a painful inflammation which is often accompanied by swelling. Jogging uphill, jogging in shoes with inflexible soles, and failure to maintain a stretching program are the three most frequent causes of achilles tendonitis. The symptoms include burning pain which usually appears early in the workout and then subsides until the run ends at which time the pain reappears and progressively worsens.

Treatment includes icing the tendon followed by gentle stretching. Prevention involves daily stretching to increase calf flexibility and the use of quality jogging shoes. Preventive maintenance is important because the tendon may tear or rupture under stress. In the latter case, surgery becomes the only effective treatment, but either situation leads to a long period of inactivity.

Shin Splints

Shin splints produce pain which radiates along the inner surface of the large bone of the lower leg. It is caused by running on hard surfaces in improper shoes. It is most prevalent among unconditioned or novice runners who do too much too soon. Jogging in one direction on a banked track or banked road shoulder can also contribute to shin splints.

Pain associated with this injury manifests itself gradually. Initially, it occurs after the workout, but as training continues, it tends to show up during the workout. In severe cases, pain may accompany walking and stair climbing. Treatment includes rest, ice applications, wrapping or taping the shin, and placing heel lifts in the shoes.

These may be supplemented by the following exercises. The Toe Flexor exercise is accomplished by sitting in a chair with the bare feet approximately shoulder width apart. Place a towel on the floor in front of both feet allowing the toes to overlap the near edge of the towel. Repeatedly curl the toes in order to pull the towel toward you so that it ends up under the arch of the feet. The heels must be in contact with the floor at all times. You may place a weight, such as a book or can of vegetables, upon the towel to increase the resistance. The Toe Extensor exercise is the reverse of the Toe Flexor. By reversing the action of the toes you will push the towel away from you and return it to the original position. Keep your heels on the floor. For the Sandsweeper exercise sit on a chair with one bare foot on the lateral edge of a towel. Grasp the towel with the toes and pivot on the heel to the right to sweep the towel in that direction. Return the foot to the starting position and repeat until the towel has been moved completely to the right. Replace the towel to the original position and sweep to the left. Repeat with the other foot.

Shin splints are nagging, painful injuries which are best prevented rather than treated. Some preventive measures include wearing quality jogging shoes, gradual adjustments to the rigors of training, avoidance of hard surfaces and hilly terrain, proper heel-toe strike, and daily use of the exercises previously described.

Chondromalacia Patella

Chondromalacia patella (chondro — cartilage; malacia — softening; patella — kneecaps) is commonly referred to as "runner's knee." This describes a condition which occurs when the kneecap tracks laterally rather than vertically during flexion and extension of the leg. Typical symptoms include soreness around and under the kneecap particularly when jogging uphill or climbing stairs. The pain must be eliminated before jogging can be safely resumed. Treatment includes rest, application of ice, and aspirin every four hours for several weeks. Ice treatment should be discontinued after 24 to 36 hours and replaced with moist heat several times per day for as long as needed.

When pain abates, the jogger may begin progressive resistance exercises to strengthen the quadriceps group (large muscles in the front of the thigh) and a low intensity graduated jogging program. Preventive measures include the use of orthotic devices (supports placed in jogging shoes to compensate for biomechanical problems which prevent abnormal motions in the foot and lower leg during jogging), jogging on soft surfaces, and abstaining from sloped or hilly terrain.

Hamstring Injuries

The hamstrings are a group of muscles in the back of the thigh. Strains and tears of the hamstrings rarely occur in health runners unless those individuals either engage in speed work or neglect to adequately stretch prior to the workout.

Hamstring injuries should be treated with rest, ice, elevation of the leg, and a firm bandage. Whirlpool bath therapy is desirable 36 hours after the injury is sustained. When the pain subsides, gentle stretching and slow jogging may be resumed.

Prevention involves daily stretching of the hamstring group. Joggers who wish to include interval training or speed work in their training program should be cautioned to gradually ease into these routines. Some researchers are advocating the use of "retro running" (running backwards) for treatment and prevention of hamstring injuries.[6] It is also being touted as a more complete warm-up than stretching. Some evidence indicates that the shock of landing each time the foot strikes the ground is equivalent to one-fourth to one-third that of forward running. Also, the position of the pelvis tends to change during retro running resulting in less stress upon the low back.

The criticisms of retro running include calf soreness and safety. One must do this form of exercise on a level terrain away from traffic, such as a running track or treadmill. More study needs to be done in this area so that more confidence can be placed in the results.

Low Back Pain

Strains which cause the muscles to spasm constitute 90 percent of all low back pain. Strains may be attributed to many varied causes but those which commonly precipitate problems for joggers are: (1) weak abdominal muscles, (2) tight low back and hamstring muscles, (3) overuse — increasing the mileage too rapidly, and (4) faulty jogging mechanics, particularly too much forward lean.

Preventive measures include daily stretching of the low back and hamstrings, strengthening of the abdominals, slowly increasing mileage, and improving faulty jogging mechanics. Jogging strengthens the muscles of the lower back; stretching exercises keep them from shortening. At the same time, the abdominal muscles need to be strengthened because they provide some support to the spinal column in holding up the weight of the torso. Treatment of low back pain includes rest, aspirin, a firm mattress with a bed board, and regular applications of heat.

Plantar Fasciitis

Occasionally, low grade pain beneath the heel of one or both feet occurs. In mild cases, the pain can be felt during jogging, but more severe cases produce pain upon walking also.[10] The pain results from microscopic tears and inflammation of the connective tissue (plantar fascia) beneath the heel. Treatment consists of cold therapy several times a day for the first few days, rest, anti-inflammatory drugs, heel pads, and possibly orthotic correction. Orthotics are supports which are placed in the running shoes which are designed to correct the biomechanical problems which may have contributed to plantar fasciitis. Prevention involves well-fitted, well cushioned jogging shoes and a stretching program which includes stretching the calf and achilles tendon. See Chapter Two.

Morton's Neuroma

Morton's Neuroma results in burning pain between the third and fourth toes usually as a result of repetitive trauma, such as that experienced by runners. Trauma is the primary cause and pain is the primary symptom. Pain is the result of scar tissue (fibrosis) impinging upon the sensory digital nerve, and may be constant or appear after walking or jogging on a hard surface. Narrow shoes, and particularly high-heeled shoes, should be avoided. Treatment may include the use of metatarsal bars or pads which are worn across the ball of the foot, shoes with a wide toebox, and local injection of a steroid preparation. Rest is suggested as long as the individual responds with pain to finger pressure at the site. If all of the above fail then surgery will be required. Prevention includes wearing shoes (jogging and everyday shoes) which are roomy in the toebox, well padded under the balls of the feet, and flexible. Jogging on softer surfaces also helps.

DOES JOGGING CAUSE ARTHRITIS?

Does the constant pounding of jogging promote premature arthritis in the joints of the legs and hips? This has been one of the persistent questions asked by joggers and those who desire to be joggers. The possibility of developing early arthritis has also provided the critics of jogging with ammunition of a persuasive nature regarding the negative effects associated with this activity.

The question of jogging's culpability in the development of arthritis was addressed by Ryan, who summarized the data from five studies in a recent issue of *The Physician and Sportsmedicine*.[7] The data from these studies indicated that there was no increase in the incidence of arthritis in active compared to inactive people. Ryan concluded that, "at present it appears that dedicated runners and other athletes are not at a greater risk of developing osteoarthritis than nonathletes."

Two excellent studies have been completed since Ryan's summary of the literature. In the first, 41 long-distance runners, age

50 to 72, were compared to 41 non-runners to determine the relationship between running and osteoarthritis (wear and tear arthritis) and osteoporosis.[8] The researchers found that the runners had 40 percent more bone mineral content than the non-runners but did not have an increase in osteoarthritis. In a second study, 17 male runners, average age of 56, and 18 male non-runners, average age of 60, were examined and compared for degenerative joint disease.[9] The researchers concluded that long-distance running was not associated with premature degenerative joint disease in the lower extremities. Further, musculoskeletal complaints focusing upon pain and swelling of the hips, knees, ankles, and feet were similar for both groups.

SUMMARY

The probability of becoming a long-time jogger is enhanced if you can avoid injury during the critical early months of the program. The way to achieve this goal is to follow the guidelines presented in this text. Injuries stifle progress, delay the attainment of program objectives, and are psychologically, as well as physically, damaging. The best way to handle injuries is to prevent them. If an injury should occur, be sure to get proper and immediate treatment. Once again, let me urge you to follow the guidelines and then let today be the first of many in your new and active life.

REFERENCES

1. Estok, P. J. and Rudy, E. B. "Physical, Psychosocial, Menstrual Changes/Risks, and Addiction in the Female Marathon and Nonmarathon Runner," *Health Care Women International*. 7, No. 3:187, 1986.

2. Powell, K. E. and others. "An Epidemiological Perspective on the Causes of Running Injuries," *The Physician and Sportsmedicine*, 14, No. 6:100, June, 1986.

3. Costill, D. L. *Inside Running*, Indianapolis: Benchmark Press, 1986.

4. Evans, W. J. "Exercise-Induced Skeletal Muscle Damage," *The Physician and Sportsmedicine*, 15, No. 1:89, January, 1987.

5. Newham, D. J. and others. "Large Delayed Plasma Creatine Kinase Changes After Stepping Exercise," *Muscle Nerve*, 6:380, June, 1983.

6. Morton, C. "Running Backward May Help Athletes Move Forward," *The Physician and Sportsmedicine*, 14, No. 12:149, December, 1986.

7. Ryan, A. J. "Exercise and Arthritis: An Encouraging Report," *The Physician and Sportsmedicine*, 9, No. 5:43, May, 1981.

8. Lane, N. E. and others. "Long Distance Running, Bone Density, and Osteoarthritis," *Journal of the American Medical Association*, 255, No. 9:1147, March 7, 1986.

9. Panush, R. S. and others. "Is Running Associated With Degenerative Joint Disease," *Journal of the American Medical Association*, 225, No. 9:1152, March 7, 1986.

10. Torg, J. S. and others. "Overuse Injuries In Sport: The Foot," *Clinics In Sports Medicine*, 6, No. 2:921, April, 1987.

The Caloric Cost Of Running

Table A.1 presents a relatively accurate estimate of the caloric cost of jogging by the mile or by the minute. Body weight and speed of running are taken into account in the calculations of the number of calories expended. Careful analysis of the table indicates that body weight is the significant factor regarding calories used; speed is insignificant.

The table was developed from data gathered on highly efficient, competitive male distance runners; therefore, the caloric expenditures shown in the various categories may actually underestimate the cost for the average jogger. Inefficient joggers may use as much as five to seven percent more calories than those noted in the table. Slightly higher caloric expenditures will also occur if jogging on a hilly course or if the weather is hot. The values in the table apply to both sexes.

To calculate the caloric cost of a workout, enter the table opposite your body weight under the appropriate speed. You will note two figures. The upper figure is the caloric cost of jogging each mile and the bottom figure represents the caloric cost per minute at that speed.

TABLE A.1.　Caloric Cost of Running*

Body Weight lbs	kgs	Running Time in Minutes Per Mile 6:00	6:30	7:00	7:30	8:00	8:30	9:00	9:30	10:00	10:30	11:00
100	45.5	65	64	64	64	63	62	62	61	61	60	59
		10.9	10.0	9.2	8.5	7.9	7.3	6.9	6.4	6.1	5.7	5.4
110	50.0	72	72	71	71	69	68	68	67	67	66	65
		12.0	11.0	10.1	9.4	8.7	8.1	7.6	7.1	6.7	6.3	5.9
120	54.5	79	78	77	77	75	74	73	73	72	71	70
		13.1	11.9	11.0	10.2	9.4	8.8	8.2	7.7	7.2	6.8	6.4
130	59.1	85	84	83	83	82	81	80	79	79	78	77
		14.2	13.0	11.9	11.0	10.2	9.5	8.9	8.3	7.9	7.4	6.9
140	63.6	92	90	90	89	88	87	86	85	85	83	82
		15.3	13.9	12.8	11.9	11.0	10.2	9.6	8.9	8.5	7.9	7.3
150	68.2	98	97	97	96	94	93	92	91	91	89	88
		16.4	15.0	13.8	12.8	11.8	10.9	10.3	9.6	9.1	8.5	8.0
160	72.7	104	103	103	102	101	99	98	97	97	96	95
		17.4	15.9	14.7	13.6	12.6	11.7	10.9	10.3	9.7	9.1	8.6
170	77.3	111	111	109	108	107	105	104	103	103	102	100
		18.5	17.0	15.6	14.5	13.4	12.4	11.7	10.9	10.3	9.7	9.1
180	81.8	117	116	116	114	113	112	112	109	109	107	106
		19.6	17.9	16.5	15.2	14.2	13.2	12.4	11.5	10.9	10.2	9.7
190	86.4	124	124	123	122	119	118	117	116	115	113	112
		20.7	19.0	17.5	16.2	14.9	13.9	13.0	12.2	11.5	10.8	10.2
200	90.9	130	129	129	127	126	124	123	122	121	120	118
		21.8	19.9	18.4	16.9	15.7	14.6	13.7	12.8	12.1	11.4	10.7
210	95.5	137	137	135	134	132	131	130	128	127	125	124
		22.9	21.0	19.3	17.9	16.5	15.4	14.4	13.5	12.7	11.9	11.3
220	100.0	144	143	141	140	138	137	136	134	133	131	130
		24.0	22.0	20.2	18.7	17.3	16.1	15.1	14.1	13.3	12.5	11.8
230	104.5	150	149	147	146	145	143	141	140	139	138	135
		25.0	22.9	21.0	19.5	18.1	16.8	15.7	14.7	13.9	13.1	12.3
240	109.1	157	156	154	153	151	150	148	146	145	143	142
		26.2	24.0	22.0	20.4	18.9	17.6	16.4	15.4	14.5	13.6	12.9
250	113.6	163	162	160	159	158	156	155	152	151	149	147
		27.3	24.9	22.9	21.2	19.7	18.3	17.2	16.0	15.1	14.2	13.4
260	118.2	170	169	167	166	163	161	160	159	157	155	153
		28.4	26.0	23.9	22.1	20.4	19.0	17.8	16.7	15.7	14.8	13.9
270	122.7	176	175	174	172	170	168	167	164	163	161	160
		29.4	26.9	24.8	22.9	21.2	19.8	18.5	17.3	16.3	15.3	14.5

Units = kcal.
Top value = Total cost per mile in kcals.
Bottom value = Cost per minute in kcals running at the speed shown.

*This chart is courtesy of Terry L. Baylor, Ph.D., Director of the Adult Fitness Cardiovascular Program at the University of Texas, Austin as it appeared in *The Essentials of Fitness*, by Falls, Baylor, and Dishman, Philadelphia: Saunders College, 1980, p. 221.

1.5 Mile Test

Aerobic capacity (max VO_2) is measured quite accurately in the laboratory with a motor-driven treadmill or bicycle ergometer along with gas collection and analysis systems. This equipment is expensive and requires considerable expertise by those doing the testing. In addition, only one subject at a time may be tested so there is a sizeable investment in time. These procedures are inappropriate for large groups; therefore, investigators have attempted to find an economical substitute which would yield accurate results.

Cooper found that the 1.5 mile run correlated very highly with treadmill tests in the measurement of aerobic capacity. It has the following advantages over laboratory testing: (1) a number of subjects can be tested at the same time, (2) it is easy to administer, and (3) the only equipment needed is a measured course and a stopwatch.

The validity and accuracy of the 1.5 mile test can be increased by allowing the subjects an opportunity to have several practice trials over the course spaced over a week or ten days. Thus, each subject becomes familiar with the course and with the pace required to produce an optimal score. After several practice trials have been allowed, each subject should attempt to run the course in the fastest possible time within his/her capacity. The most valid results are attained when subjects make an all-out effort.

The time required to cover the distance represents the score earned. Table B.1 translates the time spent to cover the distance into estimated Max VO_2 in ml O_2/kg/min. Table B.2 places the obtained Max VO_2 value into a fitness category.

TABLE B.1. 1½ Mile Run Test

Time in Minutes and Seconds	Estimated Max VO$_2$ in ml/kg/min
7:30 or less	75
7:31- 8:00	72
8:01- 8:30	67
8:31- 9:00	62
9:01- 9:30	58
9:31-10:00	55
10:01-10:30	52
10:31-11:00	49
11:01-11:30	46
11:31-12:00	44
12:01-12:30	41
12:31-13:00	39
13:01-13:30	37
13:31-14:00	36
14:01-14:30	34
14:31-15:00	33
15:01-15:30	31
15:31-16:00	30
16:01-16:30	28
16:31-17:00	27
17:01-17:30	26
17:31-18:00	25

Adapted from K. H. Cooper, "A Means of Assessing Maximal Oxygen Intake," *Journal of The American Medical Association* 203 (1968):201.

TABLE B.2 Interpretation of 1½ Mile Run Test

Age Group (yrs)	High	Good	Average	Fair	Poor
10-19	Above 66	57-66	47-56	38-46	Below 38
20-29	Above 62	53-62	43-52	33-42	Below 33
30-39	Above 58	49-58	39-48	30-38	Below 30
40-49	Above 54	45-54	36-44	26-35	Below 26
50-59	Above 50	42-50	34-41	24-33	Below 24
60-69	Above 46	39-46	31-38	22-30	Below 22
70-79	Above 42	36-42	28-35	20-27	Below 20

The average maximal O$_2$ uptake of females is 15 to 20 percent lower than that of males. To find the appropriate category for females, locate the score in the above table and shift one category to the left, e.g., the "Average" category for males is the "Good" category for females.

Adapted from J. H. Wilmore, *Training for Sport and Activity* (Boston: Allyn and Bacon, Inc., 1982).

Keeping A Progress Chart

A suggested progress chart is presented in Figure C.1. The payback for investing the few minutes required to fill out the chart pays large dividends in terms of the short- and long-term involvement received.

Weighing one's self prior to and after the workout is important, particularly in hot weather when fluid loss can become a major problem. Most of the weight lost during the workout is liquid so the difference between pre- and post-exercise weights is an approximation of the amount of fluids lost. This figure should not exceed four to five percent of the body's weight.

Over the long term, a trend for weight loss, distance, time, and jogging and resting heart rates will be discernible and the jogger will have an objective record of improvement.

FIGURE C.1. Progress Chart

Date	Weight Pre-	Weight Post-	Distance	Time	Heart Rate Jogging	Heart Rate Rest	Comments

Index